PREACHING FOR

SPIRITUAL AWAKENING

BY ROBERT F. LOGGINS, SR.

FOREWORD BY KERRY L. SKINNER

Robert F. Loggins, Sr., 15917 Eagle Chase Court, Chesterfield, Missouri 63017
Email Address: **RobertLogginsP@yahoo. com**
Website: **www. PastorLoggins. com**

Cover Design: Jay Adcock, **www.jaywilsonadcock.com**
New Logo: Kelly Nelson, Ballwin, Missouri, cover modifications and new logo.
Editing: Kerry L. Skinner (**www.kerryskinner.com**)

Printed in the United States of America

ISBN: 978-1-61658-034-6

Dedication

To my beautiful and loving wife, who is my greatest joy,
Cassandra Gail; our sons, Robert, Jr. (Beau) and
Jordan Mathia (Jay); and our wonderful and
compassionate church family,
The WORD Is Alive Ministries.

You have all granted me the great joy of service and you know
my passion for souls to be won for Christ and God's glory
as a result of what Jesus has done for us all at Calvary.
I will never be the same because of the Cross of Christ,
God's Amazing Grace, and all of you.

Contents

Foreword

Spiritual Awakening is certainly a worthy subject to study in our day! *Preaching for Spiritual Awakening* is one of the most practical ways for God's people to hear the need for revival among the people of God and for the need of spiritual awakening in our nation.

In a day when the needs of the world are being questioned by so many groups, just what really is most important? Is it the need to feed the poor, restructure government, improve public education, develop creative church plants, or change the way we budget for benevolent causes? There is no doubt that all of the former are needs and God's people should be actively involved in helping with each one. But, what is most important in our day for spiritual leaders?

Prioritizing the needs of the world is impossible for man, but not for God. So how do we discover which area of ministry is most critical for pastors, preachers, missionaries, and key spiritual leaders? Leaders must deal with personal, family, and church responsibilities daily. Balance is the issue, not priority. Leaders must balance time with family, friends, and ministry acquaintances without ignoring any of these basics in life.

The Scriptures must be our guide for knowing what messages are most critical for God's people to hear in our day. Difficult and disorienting factors can make our minds question what is most important.

God knew it would be difficult for us so, He spoke through His prophet, Jeremiah concerning prophets who had become disoriented in their duties. The spiritual leaders lost their way in how to discover the priority messages needed for God's people. God said,

> **16** *Thus says the LORD of hosts: "Do not listen to the words of the prophets who prophesy to you. They make you worthless; they speak a vision of their own heart, not from the mouth of the LORD.*
> JEREMIAH **23**:**16**

Spiritual leaders were trying to find their own way for leading the people of God. No matter what creative conferences and seminars they attended, they could not find God's way because they had become interested in their vision, not God's vision. Their messages led the people astray. Counsel from the world had overtaken their thought processes. Peace was the word they gave to the people, but there was no peace. Since the people of the world had no interest in God, the leaders did not want to oppose or expose their thinking. To do so, the prophets might not be accepted by the thinking of the day. So, God said,

> **17** *They continually say to those who despise Me, "The LORD has said, 'You shall have peace'; and to everyone who walks according to the dictates of his own heart, they say, "No evil shall come upon you."*
> JEREMIAH **23:17**

What was the missing element? God knew that the prophets had forgotten several key factors. First, they had forgotten that the people belonged to God, not the prophets. Second, they forgot that the words to be shared with the people were to be from God, not the prophets. Third, they forgot to stand in the counsel of God to receive their message. The prophets depended on the world, not God for a stirring and creative message. God made it clear when He said:

> **22** *But if they had stood in My counsel, and had caused My people to hear My words, then they would have turned them from their evil way and from the evil of their doings.*
> JEREMIAH **23:22**

May I encourage you to read this book with an open heart and mind that continues to ask God, "Is there any disorientation in my message and ministry that keeps the people of God from turning from their evil way?"

Robert Loggins has given us the messages that God put on his heart as he stood in God's counsel and received the Word to share with the people of God. Read them, reflect on them, and see if God will not stir you to learn and be more serious than ever to stand in "My [God's] counsel" and hear what you must preach in every season of life and ministry.

Dr. Kerry L Skinner
Senior Associate Pastor of Cottage Hill Baptist Church
Author of *The Joy of Repentance*
Mobile, Alabama

About the Author

Robert F. Loggins, Sr. was born in Winona, Mississippi, yet he considers Laurel, Mississippi his hometown. He received his B.S. from the University of Southern Mississippi, Hattiesburg, Mississippi; his M.Div. was earned at New Orleans Baptist Theological Seminary. Once in St. Louis, Missouri, he pursued a Doctoral of Ministry at Covenant Theological Seminary, St. Louis, Missouri. Then, due to his wife's illness, following much prayer and the healing of his wife, he was led by the Holy Spirit of God to continue his Doctoral of Ministry Program at Midwestern Baptist Theological Seminary, Kansas City, Missouri. The service of Pastor Loggins is diverse and distinctive. He has served as the pastor of The WORD Is Alive Ministries, "a disciple-making church" and the First Baptist Church of Chesterfield, both in St. Louis, Missouri. He has served as the African-American Strategist for the St. Louis Metro Baptist Association, in partnership with the Missouri Baptist State Convention, the North American Mission Board (NAMB); he has also served as the Assistant to the Director of Evangelism of the Missionary Baptist State Convention of National Baptist. He has served as a Commissioned Missionary and a Church Planter. He has written for the Evangelism Department of the Missionary Baptist State Convention of the National Baptist. He was Professor of New Testament Greek, History of The Baptist, and Philosophy at Union Theological Seminary (in partnership with New Orleans Baptist Theological Seminary, New Orleans, Louisiana). He has pastored and served churches in Mississippi, Louisiana, and now in Missouri, engaging in church planting and racial reconciliation. In conjunction with his pastoral ministry, Robert presently serves as the Prayer and Spiritual Awakening Specialist for the Missouri Baptist Convention (MBC) and the North American Mission Board (NAMB) of the Southern Baptist Convention as a Commissioned Missionary. He is known as a Bible expositor, conference speaker, and a lecturer; he serves as president of RF Loggins, Ministries, LLC and The Christian Life School of Theology and Discipleship, which are outreach, teaching, discipleship, and equipping ministries of RF Loggins, Ministries, LLC. He has gone on missionary trips in South Africa and Namibia, Africa.

He is married to Cassandra. They have two sons, Robert, Jr., and Jordan Mathia. He and his wife are the proud grandparents of a beautiful little lady,

Madison Taylor, the daughter of Robert and Christy, who live in Birmingham, Alabama.

Pastor Loggins attributes his spiritual growth and Christian development to several factors. The first factor was his mother, Gladys Louise Loggins, who raised seven children ranging in age from two-and-a-half to nineteen years, after the death of his father, Walter Loggins, Sr. The family included four girls (Doshie, Susie, Mary, and Annette) and three boys (Hoover, Walter, Jr., and Robert). The second factor in Pastor Loggins's spiritual growth and Christian development was his mother's sister, Minnie Lee Holloway.

He recalls, "Aunt Minnie taught me how to think biblically. Through her faithful life in Christ, I saw Jesus. She lived out her faith with simplicity, passion, and concern for others in both her family and her church. I learned the value and the wonderful joy of serving. Cutting lawns, visiting hospitals and prisons, helping the needy, feeding the poor and hungry were only a few things I learned from my aunt's amazing way of making Christ known; it changed my life. I decided to receive Christ as my Savior and Lord at the age of sixteen."

The third factor in Pastor Loggins's spiritual growth and Christian development was his mother's wisdom in having all her boys under the influence of godly men in their church. "I ate with the deacons, trustees, ministers, and church leaders regularly on Sundays while hanging out with my aunt, who enjoyed serving God and others. Aunt Minnie refused to take no for an answer. She even made sure that my mother and Aunt Inez participated in her ministry of service."

The final factor in Pastor Loggins's spiritual growth and Christian development was from the heart of his wife's mother, Grand Bobbye. The love I have experienced from being a member of the Burwell, Jordan, Riley, and Brewer families are beyond my ability to articulate the depths of my heart. Grand Bobby, I love you. Keep on keeping on in Jesus' name.

Acknowledgements

I want to personally thank my wife, Cassandra, for encouraging me to put this work of God into writing. She has been my friend and the love of my life for well over 30 years. She has given me two wonderful sons, Robert, Jr. (Beau) and Jordan Mathia (Jay). Beau and his wife, Christy, blessed us with two wonderful and loving grand children, Madison Taylor and Christopher Ellis Loggins.

I must also acknowledge the wonderful members of my church family, The WORD Is Alive Ministries (TWIAM). TWIAM has been the place where I have labored for well over nine years, testing the skills that the Lord has blessed me with to share with everyone I encounter in Jesus' Name.

Next, I want to acknowledge my mother, Gladys Louis Taylor Loggins; my aunt, Minnie Lee Holloway; and my wife's grandmother, Eula Burwell. All of these ladies are in the presence of the Lord. They were women of the Word. They made me better. They changed and enriched my life. By their humble transparent godly Christian example, I made the right choices to live according to God's Word!

Finally, I would like to express my joyful and heartfelt appreciation to Dr. Tom Ratcliff, the former Director of Missions for the Missouri Baptist Convention. Tom taught me how to do missions—evangelism through the power of the Holy Spirit. He was a great teacher and faithful mentor. Dr. Benny King, the former Executive Director of Missions for the St. Louis Metro Baptist Association, helped me do the impossible. Benny not only was a great teacher, he remains a great friend and brother in Christ. He opened doors for me that would have never been opened if it had not been for the person of Christ at work in his life. Last but not at all least, I want to recognize Dr. David Tolliver, Executive Director of the Missouri Baptist Convention of the Southern Baptist Convention. He is a visionary. He is a man who has a passion for people, the power of God's Word, his wife, his family, but most of all for his Lord and Savior Jesus Christ. I want to thank him personally for providing doors for me that no man can open. Thank you, Lord.

Finally, I acknowledge the God of the Bible. I acknowledge His authority. I want Him to know that I love Him more than life itself and I am compelled to preach the Word of God for His glory, honor, and praise, absent of human persuasion and personal gain.

The time is now. Brothers, we have many choices. We don't have to preach. We can choose to attempt to persuade sinners and lukewarm saints to get right with God, or we can simply preach the Word and trust God's divine intervention to change lives by the power of the Holy Spirit of God. I choose to Preach It, Brother! I have a commission from Almighty God to Preach It! And that is what I must do, lest I die. Preach! Preach! Preach!

Brothers, if you are not ready for preaching the Word to bring conviction of sin as Jesus did in Matthew 4:17, when He said, "Repent for the kingdom of heaven is at hand," then I would encourage you to put this work down immediately. God can't use a preacher who fears man more than he fears the Master. Brothers, it is either man or the Master. The choice is a matter of free will. Remember, this is not a *how-to* book; it is a *why-not* book as in *Why not preach the Word of the Living God?*

A Word about Passion

I am a man of passion. My passion is for being faithful to the Great Commission (Matt. **28:18-20**) and the Greatest Commandment (Matt. **22:37-40**). I have truly been blessed. I have the blessed honor to preach and teach the gospel of Jesus Christ each and every day of my life. What a joy it is to serve my Lord and Savior Jesus Christ. "Dear Lord God Almighty, I acknowledge You as my supreme Teacher and example in and through Your Son, The Lord Jesus Christ, Emmanuel, 'God with us.'"(Isaiah **7:14**)

Jesus Christ is the greatest preacher known to mankind. His preaching methodologies are more than templates to impress fallen humanity. He used humor, metaphors, similes, illustrations, parables, stories, and the like, but most of all He was Holy Spirit filled. It was the Holy Spirit of God in the Son of God that transformed His words into the Spirit power of gospel preaching. Jesus preached. He preached the Word in season and out of season. He rebuked. He exhorted. He corrected. He taught. He was the greatest salesman in all the world. He was the Word made flesh and dwelling among us.

So, Preach It, Brother! Preach Jesus! Preach with spirit-anointed passion for the cause of Christ. He is the only Way, the Truth, and the Life. There is no other message other than the message of the cross of Jesus Christ. If we would only keep it simple, then He achieves the complicated. When Jesus is preached, complexities are simplified. Preach It, Brother, Preach It! Preach Jesus! There is no greater name I know. Isaiah was right. Christ's passion is clearly depicted in Isaiah:

Who has believed our report? And to whom has the arm of the Lord been revealed? For He shall grow up before Him as a tender plant, and as a root out of dry ground. He has no form or comeliness; and when we see Him, there is no beauty that we should desire Him. He is despised and rejected by men, a Man of sorrows and acquainted with grief. And we hid, as it were, our faces from Him; He was despised, and we did not esteem Him. Surely He has borne our griefs and carried our sorrows; yet we esteemed Him stricken, smitten by God, and afflicted. But He was wounded for our transgressions, He was bruised for our iniquities; the chastisement for our peace was upon Him, and by His stripes we are healed. All we like sheep have gone astray; we have turned, every one, to his own way; and the Lord has laid on Him the iniquity of us all."

ISAIAH 53:1-6

So, Preach Him! Brother, Preach Him! Preach the Word and lives will be changed, hearts will be transformed, communities will be delivered, souls will be saved, and churches will flourish in the power of the Holy Spirit of God. This is the by-product of a preacher imbued with transformational passion. Transformational passion is life-changing passion.

Dr. John R.W. Stott describes this type of passionate preaching as a man who understands the authenticity of the art of true preaching. The man who preaches like this is a man like clay in the potter's hands. He is capable of standing "between two worlds," the world of dead on their way to hell and the world of the living on their way to eternal life. Dr. Stott does a masterful job in conveying the message of the definition of a preacher. He employs a variety of images to illustrate what a Christian preacher is. "The most commonest is that of the herald or town crier (kēryx), who has been given a message of good news and been told to proclaim it."[1]

The Christian preacher is not only demonstrated in the form of a herald or town crier, but the preacher is equally illustrated as a sower (speirōn).[2] He goes out into the world, like Jesus' parable of the sower, and he broadcasts the precious seed of God's Word, believing and praying that some of it will fall into the hearts of well-prepared soil and in due season will bear good fruit, fruit that will last.[3]

"[Additionally], the preacher is an ambassador (presbus)."[4] He serves as an envoy in a foreign land hostile to the truth of the gospel of Jesus Christ and he has the responsibility of representing his sovereign Lord and Savior Jesus Christ.[5]

Stott quickly adds that a sound Christian preacher is a steward or house-keeper (oikonomos).[6] His job assignment is to maintain the spiritual stability of the house by keeping it in touch with God, the Supreme Owner.

---

1 John R. W. Stott, *Between Two Worlds: The Art of Preaching in the Twentieth Century* (Grand Rapids, MI: William B. Eerdmans Publishing, 1982), 135.
2 Ibid.
3 Ibid.
4 Ibid.
5 Ibid.
6 Ibid, 136.

The final two illustrations suggest that the Christian preacher is a pastor or shepherd (poimēn),[7] that is, a good shepherd. And last but not least, the Christian preacher represents him as "one approved, a workman who has no need to be ashamed" (2 Tim. 2:15). The word used to convey this message is (orthotomeō),[8] which means "to rightly divide" the Word of God. Literally, it means to rightly take care of the business of our Father in heaven (correctly, rightly, and pleasing to Him).[9] This is transformational passion!

I have tried almost everything–yet absent of transformational passion. I have tried slick methods, special meetings, stalwart preachers, and the like. However, until Christ is clearly preached with simplicity and power, we are simply spinning our wheels in the pulpit and in the classrooms. If we are going to have an impact on the lives of sinful humanity, then we must be willing to realize that there are only two kinds of people on planet earth, the saved and the lost.[10]

Each time we preach, we are standing literally between two worlds–the worlds of the damned and the delivered. So, in order to avoid the snare of being a populist or a modern false prophet, the type of bridge to be built must be determined more by the biblical revelation than by the zeitgeist[11] or spirit of the age.[12] That is why I am urged by the urgency of the gospel to declare to all spirit-anointed preachers to preach the Word.[13]

Therefore, Preach It, Brother! Preach the Word! In season and out of seasons, preach in the courage, conviction, compassion, and commitment to God in the power of the Holy Spirit, then watch God show up and show out in this post-modern and post-Christian era (Luke 19:10).

Stott draws in the net of truth as he identifies the true source of power necessary for effective preaching, the kind of preaching that produces spiritual transformation of the human heart and soul. Stott refers to P.T. Forsyth's insight when it comes to depending either on the power of contemporary persuasion or the power of conviction through God's Holy Spirit. Forsyth begs the latter. He says:

---

7 Ibid.
8 Ibid.
9 Ibid.
10 Ibid.
11 http://dictionary.reference.com/browse/zeitgeist. *"Zeitgeist"* is a noun. It is German. It is defined as "the spirit of the time; general trend of thought or feeling characteristic of a particular period of time."
12 Ibid., 139.
13 Ibid., 141.

It is into the Bible world of the eternal redemption that the preacher must bring his people... To every age it is equally near, and it is equally authoritative for every age, however modern. The only preaching which is up to date for every time is the preaching of this eternity, which is opened up to us in the Bible alone–the eternal of holy love, grace and redemption, the eternal and immutable morality of saving grace for our indelible sin.[14]

P.T. Forsyth is on target. God's Word, the Bible, is what we need, Brothers. Our authority is not in us. It is not in theological intellect. It is solely in God's Word, the Bible. So, *Preach It, Brother! Preach the Word! Preach Jesus, crucified, risen, alive, and a soon-coming King!*

---

14 Stott, *Between Two Words*, 141.

Preface

Og Mandino, bestselling author of *The Return of the Ragpicker*, writes in his insightful and transformational work, *The Greatest Salesman in the World*, that we can change the world if we preach the right message. Mandino writes:

Who is of so little faith that in a moment of great disaster or heartbreak has not called on his God? Who has not cried out when confronted with danger, or death, or mystery beyond his normal experiences or comprehensions? From where has this deep instinct come which escapes from the mouth of all living creatures in moments of peril?[15]

As gospel preachers, we know the answer to the trilogy of questions posed by Mandino. The answer comes in the form of a triune response. Preach God the Father, the Son, and the Holy Spirit! Preach It, Brother! Preach It! This is the message that we know as believers in the Lord Jesus Christ. It is a simple phrase, "Preach Jesus! Preach the Word."

Are you ready for revival and spiritual awakening? Are you ready to see God transform communities and change lives eternally? Are you genuinely thirsty for a powerful move of God? If you are, then get ready to preach God's Word with passion, power, and persuasion. This is how I learned to preach. I learned to preach by preaching. Congregations will forgive us as preachers for a host of things, but there is one thing no preacher will be forgiven–not preaching the Word. Preaching the Word is for courageous and passionate preaching pastors, Gospel preachers, equipping teachers, and ministers of the Word of God. However, this book is not designed to help you in your preaching methods and mechanics. *Preaching for Spiritual Awakening* is written to help you, in your confidence in Almighty God, to stand up and preach "spirit-led messages,"[16] that have been anointed by the power and the person of the Holy Spirit of God to bring deep conviction, which leads to genuine repentance in the souls of all mankind. Richard Owen Roberts writes, "The first word of the gospel is not 'love.' It is not even 'grace.' The first word of the gospel is

---

15 Og Mandino, *The Greatest Salesman in the World* (New York, NY: Bantam Books, 1968), 98.

16 Greg Heisler, *Spirit-Led Preaching: The Holy Spirit's Role in Sermon Preparation and Delivery* (B&H Publishing Group: Nashville, 2007), xi.

'repent.'"[17] "From that time Jesus began to preach and to say, "Repent, for the kingdom of heaven is at hand" (Matt. **4:17**).

I am convinced, after preaching for well over three decades, that the Spirit of God will uncover the method of preaching when the Master of the Living Word of God is unveiled and unleashed with His power and our humility. The Spirit of God came alive at Pentecost before the eyes of the people of God, after they surrendered to God's will and way. We are called, commissioned, and commanded by God to do as the first church did in Acts **2**–to preach not just a *word*, but literally, the Living Word of God. Peter said, "Repent" (Acts **2:38**). So, *Preach It, Brother, Preach!* Preach the Word of God as if you have no other choice but to do it. Preach with fear as opposed to no fear. Preach with "*yârê.*" The word *yârê* means "to fear, to be afraid, to dread, or to reverence."[18]

This is not a *how-to* book; it is a *why-not* book. Why not preach the Word and trust God (Prov. **3:5-6**) with the outcome in your preaching? I have learned from personal preaching experience the necessity of the *why*? Why do I stand Sunday after Sunday and preach from the Word of God? Why did God call me to preach the Word? Why am I a gospel preacher?

The apostle Paul answers my questions with these words: "*For I am not ashamed of the gospel...*" (Romans **1:16**). R.C. Sproul asserts, "The Gospel of Jesus Christ moves to His work of atonement, affirming that Christ not only died for us, but also lived for us."[19] In brief, both Paul and Sproul agree, "God wants us to be equipped with the Word (**2 Tim. 3:16-17**). **We must trust what is inside of the Bible–the non-negotiable, inspirational, infallible, life-changing Word of God**. The Word of God works as the man of God reveals the truth of God through preaching. There is much preaching happening in our cities, in our nation, and throughout our world, but not all preaching is preached with the power and authority of the Word of God.

Powerful preaching rests on two fundamental, transformational ingredients–passion and persuasion–which bring genuine repentance. In the words of Dr. Kerry Skinner, this brings great joy. Skinner reports, "*Repentance* is the most positive word in the Bible."[20] Passion for Christ and Christ alone moti-

---

17 Richard Owen Roberts, *Repentance: The First Word of the Gospel* (Crossway Book, 2002), 23.

18 John R. Kohlenberger, III, Hebrew and Aramaic Dictionary, *"yârê,"* James Strong, *The New Strong's Expanded Exhaustive Concordance of the Bible* (Nashville, Thomas Nelson Publishers, 2001), 119.

19 R.C. Sproul, *Getting the Gospel Right: The Tie that Binds Evangelicals Together* (Grand Rapids: Baker Books, 1999), 141.

20 Kerry Skinner, *The Joy of Repentance* (Mobile, AL: Kerry L. Skinner, KLS LifeChange

vates us to this kind of preaching that brings repentance. I have learned that there is no way to true repentance other than through His "shed blood" offered on our behalf by our Lord and Savior Jesus Christ at the cross.[21]

The apostle Paul clearly understood the significance of the cross and the blood of Jesus. Thus, Paul said to the church at Corinth:

> *For the message of the cross is foolishness to those who are perishing, but to us who are being saved it is the power of God. For it is written: "I will destroy the wisdom of the wise; the intelligence of the intelligent I will frustrate." Where is the wise man? Where is the scholar? Where is the philosopher of this age? Has not God made foolish the wisdom of the world? For since in the wisdom of God the world through its wisdom did not know him, God was pleased through the foolishness of what was preached to save those who believe. Jews demand miraculous signs and Greeks look for wisdom, but we preach Christ crucified: a stumbling block to Jews and foolishness to Gentiles, but to those whom God has called, both Jews and Greeks, Christ the power of God and the wisdom of God. For the foolishness of God is wiser than man's wisdom, and the weakness of God is stronger than man's strength."*
>
> 1 CORINTHIANS 1:18-25, NIV

Paul's redemptive message was for gospel preachers who stand between the living and the dead, preaching the gospel to souls that are in need of a powerful, life-changing gospel message to call sinners to repentance. Thus, this book is written with one purpose in mind and that is to challenge preachers to preach the Word of God devoid of compromise. Don't simply preach the sweet, little, cuddly, baby Jesus of Bethlehem, but preach the supernatural, loving, crucified Jesus of Calvary. Preach all of Jesus, from cover to cover and from Genesis to Revelation. Call sin, sin. Then cry aloud in the public square that evil is evil and that God will judge the wicked and unrighteous, but He will show favor to the repentant ones as they plunge beneath the cleansing power of the blood of Jesus shed at Calvary's cross.

These are not sermons for the fearful and faint-hearted. This book is about a clear passion to preach truth in an age of human compromise and complacency. Waking the dead with the God of the Word becoming the incarnate Word—living, dwelling, moving, and flowing throughout every artery and vessel in

---

Ministries, 2006), ix.

21 Andrew Murray, *The Blood of the Cross: Christ's Blood Can Protect and Empower You!* (New Kensington: Whitaker House, 1981), 13.

the spiritual heart of the soul of mankind is the focus here. Revival preaching is not for sinners. Revival preaching is for Saints. Charles Finney declared, "When Christians become proud of their 'great revival,' it will stop."[22] Why? Pride![23] "Pride is Satan's weapon in the hearts of man."[24] Paul understood this. Paul keenly instructs his young protégé, Timothy, to simply obey God. Paul proclaims to the young man:

> *I charge you therefore before God and the Lord Jesus Christ, who will judge the living and the dead at His appearing and His kingdom: Preach the word! Be ready in season and out of season. Convince, rebuke, exhort, with all longsuffering and teaching. For the time will come when they will not endure sound doctrine, but according to their own desires, because they have itching ears, they will heap up for themselves teachers; and they will turn their ears away from the truth, and be turned aside to fables. But you be watchful in all things, endure afflictions, do the work of an evangelist, fulfill your ministry."*
> 2 TIMOTHY 4:1-5

Preach Him, Brother, Preach. Preach Jesus Christ, crucified, risen, and alive. *Preach Him, Brother! Preach* until some lost soul comes out of darkness into His marvelous light. *Preach the Good News*, until the Great Commission and the Greatest Commandments are etched on the hearts and souls of all of humanity. *Preach the WORD*!

Pastor Robert F. Loggins, Sr.

---

22 Charles Grandison Finney, *Experiencing Revival: A New Zeal for Life!* (New Kensington: Whitaker House, 1984), 83.
23 Ibid.
24 This statement is taken from an unknown author.

Chapter 1
Bring It To Jesus!

*"O unbelieving generation," Jesus replied, "how long shall I stay with
you? How long shall I put up with you? Bring the boy to me."*
MARK **9:19**, NIV

What do you do when you have given your very best effort, but nothing
changed? What do you do when you have given the best of your time, talent,
and treasure, yet the results of your investment seem to be no different? When
you have given all that you know to give, what is next?

The disciples of Jesus Christ were confronted with this problem in Mark
9:14-32. The disciple's best effort did not solve the problem even though they
had done their very best. As a matter of fact, the problem even went deeper,
darker, and lower, into the very depths of the one they were trying to help.

In Mark **9:14**, we read the masterful and meaningful biblical account of the
unique, yet perplexing event. The Bible records in Mark **9:14** these simple and
clear words, *"When they came to the other disciples, they saw a large crowd
around them and the teachers of the law arguing with them."*

When you attempt to give your best to the service of the Lord, you should
always be on guard that someone will say something negative about your actions. It does not matter how hard you work or what you do, someone will
be quick to criticize both you, and your relationship with Jesus Christ. Many
times the criticism comes from the most unexpected sources. Sometimes it
comes from those you thought really understood the Word of God.

Arguing

The Bible says in Mark **9:14** that, "The teachers of the law and a large
crowd began arguing with the disciples." The Word of God is very clear–we
as children of God must not get hung up in arguments. God tells us as His
children that we should not engage in petty arguments. Standing up for Jesus

does not require an argument. God has no trouble speaking for Himself. God does not need you to tell Him who is in His house—God already knows who is on His side.

Everyone who argues for God is not necessarily speaking for God and may not even be a child of God. Gregory R. Frizzell clarifies those who are holy and those who are not. He encourages everyone in God's house to clean up their speech. "…[s]ubtle sins of attitude and speech are often more damaging to a church than obvious outward sins."[1] With urgency, acknowledge to God that it is His house, not yours! God said in Matthew 21:13, "It is written, My house will be called a house of prayer, but you are making it a den of robbers."

The words of Jesus were penetrating when it comes to possessing an arguing spirit. Possessing an arguing spirit could rob the house of the Lord of its purpose in being a house of prayer. An arguing individual is like an armed robber entering our Father's house during Sunday morning worship and robbing our sacred worship of its spiritual legitimacy as a house of prayer. Arguing assaults authentic worship and praise in the House of Prayer—the Church of Jesus Christ. He who argues in God's house eventually causes others to pursue their individual desire as opposed to our Father's heart.

Paul instructed his young protégé, Timothy, to "Flee the evil desires." Evil desires refer to foolish and stupid arguments, quarrels and resentful spirits, unrepentant and stubborn hearts, which are all by-products of Satan's influence (2 Tim. 2:22-26).

The solution to his influence was to flee from them and to find Jesus. We must learn to avoid spending our time with things that are unproductive, destructive, and distasteful in the house of God and in the presence of Jesus Christ. Such things render God's house impotent of supernatural power.

Make it a volitional decision to pursue God's righteousness. Be a person of faith. Embrace the power of love. Build your life on the peace of God. Learn what it means to pursue righteousness, faith, love and peace with every fabric and fiber of your being. Then, calm down and watch God empower your life with the ability to witness Him as He evaporates foolish and stupid arguments like the scorching noon day sun evaporates water in the Sahara Desert.

The Bible constantly instructs us to avoid things known to produce the sins of the mouth (that is quarrels and foolish and stupid arguments). Refuse

1.Gregory R. Frizzell, *Return to Holiness, A Personal and Churchwide Journey to Revival: A Biblical Guide to Daily Cleansing and Churchwide Solemn Assemblies* (Memphis: The Master Design Ministries, 2000), 35.

to permit Satan to deceive you into engaging in superfluous personality driven activities like the disciples engaged in Mark chapter nine.

Fortunately, while the crowd and the teachers of the law were spewing disrespect, and the disciples were struggling to take authority over the demon possessed boy, Jesus spoke. Jesus is always speaking, but we must ask the question, "Do we always hear Him when He speaks to us?" In Revelation chapter three, Jesus says to the Seven Churches of Asia Minor, "He who has an ear, let him hear what the Spirit says to the churches." Jesus spoke! And when Jesus speaks, it is time to listen intently! Jesus said in Mark **9:16**, "Why are you arguing?" In other words, *"What in the world is wrong?"* Something must be wrong. Why? Because it was consistently clear and penetrating with powerful, prophetical, life-changing truth, that God's people were arguing and disrespecting each other. Something is deeply wrong when you are in the presence of Jesus with an argumentative spirit!

In the midst of Jesus' probing question, the father of the demon possessed son said, "Teacher, I brought you my son…but your disciples could not drive out the spirit." The father was concerned with what the spirit was doing to his son. His son was robbed of speech. Each time he sought to utter a word, the spirit of evil choked out his voice. The son was not only robbed of speech but he was seized and thrown to the ground by the same spirit. Once the spirit threw him to ground, foam spewed from his mouth as he gnashed his teeth and became rigid like a first century statue of a Greek god. The father informed Jesus that he had consulted his disciples but they were unable to drive out the spirit of evil. The father said to Jesus, "…but they could not" (Mark **9:17-18**, TNIV).

It wasn't that the disciples did not want to cast out the demon–they could not do it. Their failure was due to possessing proper authority. The disciples had power, but they did not possess the authority from God to cause their power to be effective. Taking authority is the key in dealing with evil spirits. Evil spirits know and realize the presence of effectual power which possesses authority. This is known as supernatural intervention. Supernatural intervention means more than saying words and utilizing your rote memory. Divine intervention evokes heavenly power to achieve earthly work. The disciples employed improper power. Improper power always results in human failure and disappointment. According to the story in Mark **9:18**, the Scripture records these words, "…but they [the disciples] could not." They could do what they believed they were capable of doing. So, arguing showed up.

The people believed they had a reason to be arguing. They had asked the disciples to help but they could not! No wonder the father was so perplexed. The disciples of Jesus had failed them at a very critical, crucial, and difficult time of need. The father needed help and the very men who had been with the Son of God Himself had failed. The disciples failed. They could not help. They could not perform this one major miracle.

No wonder the disciples were so disappointed, dejected, defeated, and distraught. Although they were empowered with the living truth and the authority of the Living Word, the Lord Jesus Christ had resources and power that they did not understand. The disciples stood face to face with an evil that looked them directly in their eyes and refused to release a father's son from demonic control and spiritual oppression. This time they failed.

This Kind of Spirit

Although Jesus had told them (the disciples), *"You can do it,"* the disciples were faced with something much more complex, complicated, confusing, cunning, and clever than they were. The disciples were faced with a *"This kind of spirit"* They came to the place where they concluded they could not handle *"this kind of spirit."* Have you ever come in contact with a *this kind of spirit*? Have you ever come in contact with something so deep, dark, and ugly that you did not know what to do?

This was one demon that they could not handle in the power of human ability and presumed untested divine power afforded to them through the person of the Christ. They had handled many other demons before, but this demon was wicked, evil, and deceptive all at the same time.

The disciples were totally perplexed. So what did they do? What would you do? Would you have run for your life? Would you pull out heavy weapons and sound the attack to take a "Custer's Last Stand" approach? What would you do?

Deciding to do what all committed believers in the power and provisions of God should and must do in times of great challenge and demonic encounters, the disciples must–*Bring it to Jesus!* When you are perplexed and are dealing with a situation that you can't handle, just–*bring it to Jesus!* Just *bring it to Jesus! Tell Jesus all about it! Bring it to Jesus!* As a matter of fact, *bring all of it to Jesus!*

The Bible says in Mark **9:20**, "So they brought him. When the spirit saw Jesus, it immediately threw the boy into a convulsion. He fell to the ground and rolled, foaming at the mouth." Then, in Mark **9:25**, Jesus, the miracle worker who can do anything but fail, "...rebuked the evil spirit." Jesus said with a boldness, "You deaf and mute spirit, I command you, come out of him and never enter him again." Immediately, the spirit shrieked, convulsed him violently and came out" (Mark **9:26**, NIV).

Whenever the presence of evil and darkness collides with the power and authority of light, darkness takes its flight. The darkness of evil flees from the light of the Lord. When the light of the Lord covers darkness of evil, darkness has to pack its bags and take the next flight out of town. Mark **9** revealed this.

Yet, everyone assumed that the boy was dead. He was not dead. He was simply preparing to live for the first time in his life. Jesus took the young man by his hand and lifted him to his feet. Immediately, he stood up. Jesus healed him. He was a changed man.

There is an old African–American colloquialism that says, "Kan't nobody due me like Jesus!"[2] Only Jesus can lift you up, and keep you up. People can lift you up, but eventually they will let you down. Jesus, however, will lift you up and keep you up and He will never let you down! The Bible states that Jesus healed this demon-possessed young man. Jesus ran the evil spirit out of him.

Wouldn't it be great today if Jesus would just show up at your church and literally run everything that is not of Him out of your church? I wonder how many folks would start going into convulsions, start violently shaking, and fall like dead men. I wonder how many ungodly, evil, unrighteous spirits and attitudes enter into the House of God each and every Sunday. All of us have an evil thought or demonstrate an evil attitude every now and then. If it had not been for the Lord on our side, there is absolutely no telling what we would do. But thank God for Jesus and thank God for the power of the Holy Spirit of God. He is the only one that is able to keep us from killing ourselves and causing us to miss all the blessings that God has in store for our lives.

Christ's disciples could not handle this problem. In the same way, the disciples of a local congregration may not be able to handle a problem like this either because "disciples are made, not born."[3] The disciples did not realize that "Discipleship is our opportunity to tap the infinite resources of God."[4] These resources are supernatural in equipping us to present the gospel of Jesus Christ with power beyond our human capacity. This supernatural equipping

2 Cultural slang.
3 Walter A. Henrichsen, *Disciples Are Made Not Born: Equipping Christians to Multiply Themselves Through Ministry to Others* (Wheaton, IL: Victor Books, 1974), 8.
4 Ibid., 31.

by the Holy Spirit is the doorway where Spirit-filled preaching, teaching, and deliverance enter.

The disciples failed to visualize the door. But I know a man. I know a man who can open the door to handle *this kind of spirit.* I know a man who can handle (as in Romans **1:29-30**) every kind of wickedness, evil, greed, and depravity. He can handle every kind of envy, murder, strife, deceit, and malice. He can handle all the gossips, slanderers, all the God-haters, the insolent, arrogant, boastful, disobedient–all those who are senseless, faithless, heartless, ruthless. He can handle all of those who, act as if they intuitively possessed an experiential knowledge of God that was dropped from heaven itself. Yet in reality their knowledge of God is impotent of God's righteousness. It was evident in their behavior. "Although they know God's righteous decree," yet they chose to do as they pleased. Although they understood exactly what God said, they chose to do the exact opposite of what God had decreed.

Self-pleasure usurped self-denial. Not only did they continue to do what pleased themselves, they taught others to practice disobedience as well. God's righteous decrees were nothing more than words in the cartoon section of the local newspaper. In other words, approving the things that God disapproved brought greater joy than disapproving the things that God disapproved. They were no different than the struggling disciples (Rom.**1:32**, NIV).

However, the disciples did what each of us must do, even right now while you are reading this book on this exact date in our lives–*Bring it to Jesus!* But even after bringing it to Jesus, they were still wondering, they were still perplexed and confused. They wanted to know why, after all the things they had done before, *"Why couldn't we drive out this kind of evil spirit?"*

"Master," they said, *"Why couldn't we drive this demon out of the boy? Why could we do it this time?"* The disciples were embarrassed and perplexed. They were dealing with the devil. The crowd was probably laughing at them. "When the spirit of modernity seeps into the underground water supply to the heart of the believer, confusion and compromise contaminate our fresh water supply."[5] Flirting dangerously with modernity can cripple the work of the Lord.[6]

People tend to expect you to be superhuman when you say that you are a child of God. If they observe you having a difficult time with a problem, they

---

5 Os Guinness, *Dining with the Devil: The Megachurch Movement Flirts with Mordernity* (Grand Rapids, MI: Baker Book House, 1993), 21.
6 Ibid.

mock you by saying, "I thought you were a Christian!" Possibly the crowd was saying, "*Well, I knew they could not do it. I knew they did not have what it takes to deal with this bad, dark, deadly, ugly, nasty, grizzly, greasy, boastful, sneaky, disrespectful, dirty, backbiting, backstabbing evil and wicked demon.*"[7]

Possibly the crowd said in the marketplace, "*We have seen this big, bad demon defeat many disciples. We have witnessed this one demon run off many godly disciples and god-fearing, nice, kind and sweet disciples. We have seen this one big demon distract people, disrespect God's holy name and even disrespect the very Word of God and the work of the kingdom of God.*"

The crowd surely concluded with these stinging words: "*Well, it looks like nobody can cast out this evil spirit.*" So the crowd more than likely concluded, "*Well, another one bites the dust.*" But there was something the crowd did not realize–these disciples were disciples of Jesus Christ, God's only begotten Son! They failed to realize, "Prayer is powerful. Prayer not only changes things, prayer changes the one who is praying."[8] E.M. Bounds, in his classic work on prayer, pens an entire chapter on "Prayer Miracles."[9] He says, "The miracle of miracles in the earthly career of our Lord, the raising of Lazarus from the dead, was remarkable for its prayer accompaniment."[10] Jesus did not pray to convince God, He prayed to console man. "Jesus lifted up His eyes, and said, Father,"[11] Don't do this for Me. Do it for those who see and yet remain blind. Do it for their faith. Bounds reports, "It was a prayer mainly for the benefit of those who were present, that they might know that God was with Jesus because God had answered His prayers."[12] Someone has said, "Prayer works, when you work prayer."[13] The real issue is not what we do but it is the God who answers prayer that is the key to power.

However, the disciples knew God–they knew Him as God Almighty, Adonai, Jehovah, Elohim, Prince of Peace, the Great Physician, the Savior, the Word made flesh, Lord, the Light of the World, the Lifter of Men, the Lamb of God, the Head of the Church, the Chief Cornerstone, etc.[14] The disciples were no pushovers. They knew God. They knew God's handiwork. Yet the disciples

7 Ibid.

8 Robert F. Loggins, Sr., *The Journey to Wholeness & Holiness: Fasting and Prayer* (Chesterfield, MO: RF Loggins Ministries, 2007), 112.

9 E. M. Bounds, *E. M. Bounds: The Classic Collection on Prayer* (Orlando: FL: Bridge-Logos, 2001), 262.

10 Ibid, 263.

11 Ibid.

12 Ibid.

13 An unknown author.

14 Lambert Dolphin, *The Names of God.* www.ldolphin.org/Names.html.

wanted to know why they could not drive out this one evil spirit in a little boy in Mark **9:28**.

Jesus then told His disciples in so many words that, *"Yes, I have given you power. I have given you power. But I want you to know something very critical and very important. The reason why you could not do this great thing is simple. You have not been trusting in Me. I have given you the authority in "My Name." So use it! Use what I have given to you. Don't be fearful or afraid. Trust Me and let me work the work of grace in and through your very being.* But they did not. The disciples missed Discipleship 101. They must have been sleeping. And they failed to drive out the "this kind of spirit in the boy!"

Jesus said, "This kind of spirit will only come out by prayer and fasting!" That's the only way you can handle it! "This kind can come out only by prayer and fasting!" In other words, Jesus is saying, *It is possible, but you must be willing to get down on your knees, bow your head and put away eating and focus on the authority and the Divine Righteousness and Holiness of God's Eternal Power to do the full job.*

Jesus taught the disciples the principle of mutual compatibility. Mutual compatibility in the context of prayer and fasting required a merger of one's principle (i.e., faith in God) and practice (i.e., obedience in God). Disciples of Christ had to learn how to merge what they believed with what they could do. One's actions are connected to one's faith. The writer of Hebrews proclaims, "Without faith it is impossible to please God" (Heb. **11:6**, NIV). Paul declares, "For we walk by faith and not by sight" (**2** Cor. **5:7**, NIV). "Now faith is the substance of things hoped for, the evidence of things not seen" (Heb. **11:1**, KJV). Faith requires action. Action is simply what we do. Faith and action are mutually compatible.

Mutual compatibility of faith and action was one of the goals of Jesus' teaching on prayer and fasting. To authenticate their power they had to have been with Jesus. They had indeed been with Jesus physically, but they had not identified with Jesus by faith. The disciples were walking with Jesus but they had not fully embraced His teaching. They understood Jesus as a rabbinical teacher but Jesus was much more than that.

Understanding who and whose we are is critical in reaping the blessing and benefits of faith and action. Do you remember the Lord's conversation with Solomon in **2** Chronicles **7**? The Lord said, "If My people." If God's people. These were people who were sensitive to the voice of God. God whispered and they heard Him. God's people were eager to hear what He had to say. Carnality creates a spiritual thrombosis, whereas humility, prayer, seeking God's face, turning from our wicked ways affords us to hear what God says. Faith demands action. Obeying demands doing. Once again this is the principle of mutual compatibility.

Hearing from heaven will never happen apart from embracing humility, prayer, seeking God's face, and turning from our wicked ways. Heaven is broadcasting spiritual insights even as you read and study what it means to preach for spiritual awakening. Heaven's message was clear. The heart of the disciples was the problem. The Spirit of God flows freely when faith intersects action. Mutual compatibility of faith and action is the key.

God called His people to demonstrate humility which leads to healing. Prayer and fasting ignited a revival in the Old Testament story and prayer and fasting illustrated a new paradigm in the disciple making ministry of Jesus. Authentic discipleship occurs when our faith and action are mutually compatible. Then, God not only heals a demon possessed boy, but He also heals the soil of our souls (2 Chronicles 7:14, NIV).

Jesus healed the boy. God desires to heal us as well. The land or the soil was identified in Genesis Chapters 1 and 2 as the source of life. Life occurred in Genesis Chapters 1 and 2 at the very moment when God breathed His life into the lifeless lump of clay. Jesus took the lump of clay and the young man got up and walked. Obviously this was God's desire for Israel in 2 Chronicles 7:14.

Casting out this evil spirit required the disciples and will require us to bring it to Jesus by fasting and praying. Notice what Jesus said: "This kind can come out only by prayer and fasting." But what is *this kind?* A–*this kind of spirit*–is so deep, dark, deadly, and deceptive. How do you know how to identify the source of this spirit? The Bible says, "Let the wheat and the tares grow together, and Jesus said when the time comes, He would do the separating." But the Word also says, in Matthew 12:33, "That you know that tree by the fruit it bears." And Matthew 12:35 says, "A good man brings good things out, but a bad man brings bad things out." So what is *this kind of spirit?*

This kind of spirit in the church of Jesus Christ is hard to understand. It is not the Spirit of God. God's Spirit is holy.[15] You cannot deal with *this kind of spirit* with more knowledge or more human understanding. *This kind of spirit* in the church of the Jesus Christ is very confusing and perplexing. *This kind of*

---

15 J. I. Packer, *God's Words: Studies of Key Bible Themes* (Grand Rapids, MI: Baker Book House, 1981), 171.

spirit can quote many Bible upside down, and reject living out the Bible right side up. *This kind of spirit* can teach and lead in Bible study and appear to be an excellent teacher, but will cut you down with the tongue and embarrass you publicly as if you have never read the Bible. *This kind of spirit* even has the audacity to recite and read the *Church Covenant*, Sunday after Sunday without ever changing! *This kind of spirit* believes *It* knows more than God about what God should have said or written in the Living Word of God. But, *It* never lives what it says *It* declares *It* knows innately.

What must one do to banish *this kind of spirit*? We must bring it to Jesus! Only Jesus can do it. Only Jesus can heal the sick, raise the dead, cast out evil spirits, open blinded eyes, heal the wounded heart, make things that can't and won't happen, come to complete fruition. Only Jesus has the power and the authority to do it.

Time To Change

Is there anything hindering your message and your ministry? Are you confronted with a *this kind of spirit* where you are laboring for God? Are you on the verge of giving up? Have you already thrown in the proverbial towel?

If you are at this point, I have some good news for you today. The Lord has planted within you the supernatural ability to do all things through Christ who strengthens you. The Lord has filled you with authority and power. The Lord is your Shepherd and you shall not want. The Lord is your life and your salvation, who shall you fear and of whom shall you be afraid. Beloved, the Lord is with you. Now, what He wants you to do is quite simple and that is *Bring it to Him*! If we would only release it into the Master's hands, we would experience a divine breakthrough. God will burst open the dam of disappointment and deliver us safely on the other side of joy, peace, patience, love, and success.

The Bible is clear. What Jesus commanded His disciples to do with the evil-spirit-possessed boy is what He did when He confronted death, hell, and the grave at Calvary. Jesus brought it to His Father. He said, "Father, into Thy hands I commit my Spirit." Then the Bible says, "He gave up the ghost and He died." He died until the dead got up. He died until the dividing wall of the curtain in the temple was removed. He died until His death defeated death itself.

On Resurrection Sunday morning, the Lord Jesus Christ got up with all power in His hands. Jesus is Alive! The Word is Alive! He lives! He lives! He lives! Homer A. Rodeheaver, in 1933, penned these words for our edification:

I serve a risen Savior, He's in the world today; I know that He is living, whatever men may say; I see His hand of mercy, I hear His voice of cheer, And just the time I need Him He's always near. He lives, He lives, Christ Jesus lives today! He walks with me and talks with me along life's narrow way. He lives, He lives, salvation to impart! You ask me how I know He lives? He lives within my heart.[16]

16 "He Lives," Copyright 1933 by Homer A. Rodeheaver. Renewed 1961. The Rodeheaver Company. All Rights Reserved. Used by Permission. Alfred H. Ackey. Number 102 in the *National Baptist Hymnal* (Nashville: National Baptist Publishing Board, 1977), 102.

Chapter 2

The Holiness of God

And they were calling to one another: "Holy, holy, holy is the LORD Almighty; the whole earth is full of his glory." "Woe to me!" I cried. "I am ruined! For I am a man of unclean lips, and I live among a people of unclean lips, and my eyes have seen the King, the Lord Almighty."

ISAIAH **6:3, 5**, NIV

When will God send revival? There are numerous fundamental prerequisites to an effective prayer life. One of the many fundamental prerequisites to an effective prayer life is revealed to us in the dynamic nature of embracing the critical necessity of the holiness of the God who is holy. If we become literally consumed by the power and presence of Almighty God, then we fall prey to Luther's insanity. Martin Luther declared, "Love God? Sometimes I hate Him."[1] This is an unusual account of a man who is considered as one of the stones in the foundation of the church. Luther, restricted by the circumstances of his humanity, further laments, "Sometimes Christ seems to me nothing more than an angry judge who comes to me with a sword in His hand."

Luther, desperate for life or death, debates with God's holiness. Luther's tempestuous behavior surfaces at the Lord's Supper. He pounds his fist on the table of the Lord and bellows over and over, again and again, "*Hoc est corpus meum, hoc est corpus meum*." ("This is my body. This is my body.")[2] Here is a godly man utterly frustrated with himself and his sinful condition could not change himself.

Hundreds of years before Martin Luther, God commissioned a major prophet with a major message. The prophet Isaiah wrote his prophetic message despite Assyrian domination. God always has a man who is willing to obey God in

---

1 R.C. Sproul, "The Insanity of Luther," Chapter 5, *The Holiness of God* (Wheaton, IL: Tyndale House Publishers, Inc., 1985), 101.
2 Ibid, 102.

difficult times. Isaiah was that man because he came to understand the critical necessity of the holiness of God, despite the brutality of King Tiglath-Pileser III and the oncoming bondage of the people of God.[3] Isaiah became a changed man. The year is 740 BC.

Isaiah saw the Lord. He did not simply see a reflection of the essence of the Lord, he saw the exalted nature of the Lord. The Lord was in a position of power and authority. Preaching for spiritual awakening draws its power and authority from the power and authority of the exalted King, the Lord God Almighty. Isaiah saw the Lord. Seeing the Lord was not something that Isaiah boasted of to others. He sought to tell his story. When we preach the Word of God with the Spirit's power it brings people into a deeper inner life change in Christ. Inner life change goes beyond what is seen to that which is not seen. Inner life change focuses on the human soul. Preaching for spiritual awakening in this venue creates new creations. If any man or woman be in Christ old things continue passing away as new things become newer (2 Cor. 5:17).

Isaiah saw the Lord. His God was seated on His throne. He was lifted up. His influence, as denoted by the train of His robe, saturated the temple both physically and spiritually. Our bodies are the spiritual temples of the presence and power of God (1 Cor. 6:19). Isaiah understood what we must come to understand today in this fallen world. Don't attempt to bring Jehovah God, the exalted LORD, down to our sinful human level. The Lord's presence was esteemed. Angelic beings were celebrating, "Holy, holy, holy is the LORD Almighty; the whole earth is full of his glory." God was everywhere.

Preaching for spiritual awakening creates an atmosphere of hope and anticipation. Hope points to the future in general. Anticipation points to hope that has been defined at a given specific point in time. Given the magnitude of this supernatural encounter Isaiah experienced God in a totally new way. "Woe to me! He cried. I am ruined! He cried out." I am a man like David, unclean. Isaiah interfaced his inadequacy with the inadequacy of King David. Isaiah saw his hopelessness as King David came to realize his hopelessness. He was hopelessly unclean. His lips were like the people God had instructed him to prophesy to for the purpose of bring them deliverance. The deliverance he preached was the deliverance he needed most. Although he lived among a people with unclean lips, he saw what no other human being could see. He saw the King, the Lord God Almighty.

---

3 William Hendriksen, *Survey of the Bible: A Treasury of Bible Information* (Grand Rapids, MI: Baker Books, 1976), 112.

Then one of the angelic beings flew to him with a sizzling hot coal in his hand, taken from the fire of the altar of God and touched his lips. At that moment Isaiah's sin was atoned. Now Isaiah was ready to help his people. God's message was clear now. God said, "Whom shall I send? And who will go for us?" Isaiah heard and understood the message with a keener insight. Then he said, "Here am I. Send me!"

Encountering God's power and presence changed Isaiah. God's message was clear in 2 Chronicles 7:14. God wanted all His messengers to understand the message before they communicated the message. The message was clear. Isaiah communicated the message. Israel had a choice. Israel could reject or accept the message of revival and avert retribution. (Isaiah 6:1-8, NIV).

That is why Isaiah 6:3 said, "And they were calling to one another: 'Holy, holy, holy (that is Qadosh, Qadosh, Qadosh)[4] is the Lord Almighty; the whole earth is full of His glory.'"[5] Isaiah realized one of the key fundamental prerequisites for an effective prayer life is understanding that God is holy. Holy, Holy, Holy God is holy. Isaiah encountered the holiness of God.

Our Awesome God

A.W. Tozer, in his work, *The Knowledge of the Holy*, uttered these most insightful and life-changing words to those of us who are interested in who God is and are captivated by the awesomeness of God's splendor and wonderment. These words are "What we believe about God is the most important thing about us."[6]

The word *God* itself is one of the most widely used terms in our language, yet it is nebulous and undefined in most human minds today. However, for the faithful believer in the Lord Jesus Christ, Almighty God is transcendent, that is He excels above all. He has no limits. He is not bound to physical boundaries. Nothing in the heavens above or the earth beneath possesses the inherent power to limit or restrain what He and only He can do within Himself.

In addition to His transcendence, God is imminent, that is He is ever near. One can whisper and it literally shouts in the throne room of God. His presence and power pervade the whole of creation. Draw nigh to God and He will draw

---

4 K. Elliger and W. Rudolph, *Biblia Hebraica Stuttgartensia* (Stuttgart: Deutsche Bibelgesellschaft Stuttgart, 1983), 684.

5 Isaiah, 6:3 coveys the message of God's Holiness in the Hebrew expression, "Qadosh, Qadosh, Qadosh", see the Hebrew Bible, *Biblia Hebraica Stuttgartensia*, 684.

6 http://www.amazon.com/gp/offer-listing/1850786216/ref=sr_1_olp_1?ie=UTF8&s=books&qid=1255670161&sr=8-1.

nigh to thee. Our God is near. Not only is God near, He is omnipotent, that is all-powerful (Romans **1:19-20**; Jeremiah **32:17**; Luke **1:37**, Hebrews **6:18**).[7] God is omnipresent, that is to say, He is in all places, all the time. God is omniscient, that is to say, He knows everything.[8] In Isaiah **46:9-10**, God said this about Himself, "I am God, and there is no other; I am God, and there is none like Me. I make known the end from the beginning." In other words, "Nothing surprises God." God is immutable, that is to say, He will never change.[9] He is unassailable, indisputable, undeniable, and absolute in the totality of His Divine Essence.

God is eternal, that is to say, He is timeless. He never had a beginning and will never have an end. God is infinite, that is to say, He is unlimited in time, space and/or matter.[10] God is unchangeable, that is to say, He does not vary or waver at all. James **1:17**, NIV says, "who does not change like shifting shadows."

God is personal; that is to say, He is a person. God is Love; His love is perfect love.[11] God is one in Three Persons: Father, Son and Holy Spirit.[12] God is Holy. Lord, Send a Revival and Let It Begin with Me...

God is unlimited, near, all-powerful, and everywhere. God has all wisdom and He never changes. God is eternal and has no boundaries.[13] God is unchangeable, He is love, and is Triune: Father, Son and Holy Spirit, God is Holy, and God is Our Best Friend.[14]

That is why, in Isaiah **6:3** (NIV), the seraphs shouted these words in splendor and reverence of God. "Holy, holy, holy is the Lord Almighty; the whole earth is full of His glory." Through the book of Isaiah, we enter into the presence of God, for five chapters or for 115 verses. Isaiah was caught up in a vision. In Isaiah **1:1**, NIV, the Bible says, "The vision concerning Judah and Jerusalem that Isaiah son of Amoz saw during the reign of Uzziah, Jotham, Ahaz and Hezekiah, kings of Judah." In that day our Heavenly Father spoke concerning a day in which "the Branch of the Lord will be beautiful and glorious." It was "the Branch of the Lord." The Branch of the Lord is an analogy of Israel. Israel is described as being beautiful and glorious. Israel's productivity captured God's attention.

7 David Noel Freedman, "Names and Attributes of God," *Eerdmans Dictionary of the Bible* (Grand Rapids, MI: William B. Eerdmans Publishing Company, 2000), 510–517.

8 Ibid., 32.

9 Ibid.

10 Ibid.

11 Ibid.

12 Ibid.

13 Ibid.

14 Ibid., 33.

Preaching for spiritual awakening seeks to increase the productivity, faithfulness, dignity, and beauty to the people of God. The Branch of the Lord was identified as a fruit bearing branch. God referred to the productive branch as holy. God elevated His people. He provided cleansing, productivity, direction, shelter, and a hiding place from the hard and difficult times. That was why Isaiah said, "In that day the Branch of the Lord will be beautiful and glorious, and the fruit of the land will be pride and glory of the survivors in Israel" (Isaiah 4:2-6, NIV).

God declared to His chosen people, "I will never forget about you, nor let you down. I will always leave a branch. I will always be your God and you will always be my people. This was God's eternal promise to Israel forever. God was trustworthy.

In the midst what God promised, the hope of Isaiah died at the death of King Uzziah. The kings of men had to die before Isaiah saw the King of kings and the Lord of lords. The King of kings and the Lord of lords never shares His glory with the king of men. Uzziah died and Isaiah saw the Lord. Seeing the Lord requires having a clear visual path. The sightline of the prophet of Isaiah was once obstructed but now he was capable of clear sight into the throne room of God. Isaiah not only saw the Lord, he felt His presence, and heard His voice through spirit beings (Isaiah 6:1-4, NIV).

In other words, the Lord showed up and the people recognized His presence! God's manifest presence will result in Greater Power, Greater Blessings, Greater Love, Greater Compassion, Greater Faithfulness, Greater Determination, Greater Healing, Greater Soul Winning, Greater Baptismal Services, Greater Outreach, Greater Ministries, Greater Giving, Greater Sharing and Greater Holiness. When this happens, the church and all her people become a Greater Blessing as a Greater People in the Kingdom of God saying, "Holy, holy, holy, the whole earth is filled with His glory!" But, this will not happen unless we see ourselves as God sees us. Uzziah had to die.

Let's review what Isaiah experienced. Isaiah saw himself the way God saw him. Isaiah said, "Woe to me! I am ruined! For I am a man of unclean lips, and I live among a people of unclean lips, and my eyes have seen the King, the Lord Almighty" (Isaiah 6:5, NIV).

What was it that caused Isaiah to see himself? Isaiah saw the Holiness of God. Isaiah 6:4 said, "Holy, holy, holy…" Three Holies! I believe that the first holy refers to His name–God is Holy–The Father.

Psalm **111:9** (NIV) said, "...holy and awesome is His name." Luke **11:2** (NIV) states, "...hallowed be Thy Name..." John **16:24** (NIV) said, "...asked for anything in My name..." Philippians **2:10** (NIV) revealed that, "...at the name of Jesus every knee should bow..." Revelation **19:13** (NIV) said, "...and His name is the Word of God. Holy and Awesome is His Name." The first holy referred to His name.

His names revealed His nature and character. God never changes. "He is the same yesterday and today and forever" (Heb. **13:8**, NIV). God never changes and we can trust Him. We can trust in the Lord with every fabric and fiber of our being. God has commanded us to completely trust Him. (Prov. **3:5-6**). The first holy referred to God's name–God is Holy–The Father. There was yet another holy.

I believe that the second holy referred to His nature–God is Holy–the Son. Joshua **24:19** (NIV) said, "...He is a holy God..." Paul agreed with Joshua's theology declaring the holiness of God. In Paul's Epistle to the church at Rome, he punctuated his apostolic theological argument concerning the nature of God's holiness. He boldly spoke without apology words of truth concerning man's decadence and the Savior's divinity.

Listen now to the heart of Paul as the Bible reported on God's New Testament reaction to sinful man blinded by sin and selfishness. What happened when the spirit of Uzziah refused to die and obstructs the sightline to the glory of God?

"But God showed His anger" (Rom. **1:18**, NIV). God's anger was hurdled from heaven against all sinfulness and weaknesses of men. Wickedness sought to cover the truth about God. Truth was ignored although it was obvious to the wicked heart. God's anger fell because man's excuses were not accepted by God. Why? The hearts of men were cold and hard. Worship was substituted by humanism and foolish ideas of true worship was jaded. Preaching for spiritual awakening is God's way of using mortal man to communicate biblical truth to the wicked, wayward, and wondering generation back to God.

Although profound truth was presented, the hearts and minds of the wicked reminded darkened and confused. The Scripture said, they claimed to be wise in their own ways and thus their foolishness usurped potential faith in God. God decided to leave them alone. God departed. When God abandoned man to his own ways, hell's pit spewed up a gushing flow of filth and unwholesomeness. Like an erupting volcano, dormant for hundreds of years, came forth God's wrath upon every kind of wickedness, sin, greed, hate, envy, murder, quarrelling, deception, malicious behavior, and gossiping spirit. Then, without warning like a Tsunami, a tidal wave of God haters, insolent spirits, backstabbing hearts, prideful and boastful sinful spirits promoted themselves above God, because God had abandon them to their own way of thinking and doing things.

The second holy, the nature of God, regrettably was ignored because the spirit of Uzziah refused to die in the hearts of men. Preaching for spiritual awakening calls men and women to die. Life in Christ requires death in Christ. No death! No life! "I have been crucified with Christ and I no longer live, but Christ lives in me" (Gal. 2:20, NIV). The crucified life is a life of personal choice. Personal choice was connected to personal holiness in Paul's teaching to both the Romans Christians and the Christians scattered throughout Asia Minor and Galatia. Uzziah must die.

Paul concluded his letter to the Roman Christians by saying, that they knew God's justice requirement–those who do these things deserve to die, yet they do them anyway. Worse yet, they encourage others to do them too. This can happen to us as well when we deny the second holy of God–that was His nature. God is Holy and we are not.

The preacher must be a changed man. Both his nature and his name must change. Death was the demand for such change. Uzziah had to die. Metaphorically the death of Uzziah was an illustration of the preacher's name and nature. He is now ready to experience a third change, which was a change in propinquity to God.

The third holy refers to His nearness. God is holy–the Holy Spirit. Ezekiel 20:41 says, "I will show Myself holy among you..." *I* refers to God. *Will* speaks to the God's timing. What is Ezekiel saying? He is saying that God in His infinite wisdom and in His Spirit power will accomplish His ultimate task. He will produce nearness. Nearness implies God's presence and power to deal with the heart of sinful man. This is where pride and peace is separated by humility and holiness. We know God is near when the spirit of humility is elevated above the spirit of pride. Listen to James as he drives home his point on the nearness of God. Let us never forget that God is near!

James makes a great distinction in holiness by contrasting the proud from the humble. He boldly addresses it as a matter of a spiritual fight. He argues that there is a profound difference between pride and humility. James said, "What is the source of the wars and fights among you?" James sought to help the church community uncover its heart true passion. The third holy–its nearness is a battle between pride and humility. The battle between pride and humility was the battle confronting the New Testament Church Diaspora in Asia Minor. The battle has not changed today.

Immediately, James addressed the wars and fights in the church. These were not physical battles and wars. He was speaking of spiritual strife resulting in church fights within the hearts of men and without the acts of men's hearts. Rhetorically, James questioned the church members. Don't your fights and wars come from an inner war in you? You want something you can't get. You will never get it because you refused to ask God. The church had a desire problem. Unfortunately it has not changed today. We are still in a similar condition as the New Testament Church Diaspora.

> *What is the source of the wars and the fights among you? Don't they come from the cravings that are at war within you? You desire and do not have. You murder and covet and cannot obtain. You fight and war. You do not have because you do not ask. You ask and don't receive because you ask wrongly, so that you may spend it on your desires for pleasure.*

> *Adulteresses! Do you not know that friendship with the world is hostility toward God? So whoever wants to be the world's friend becomes God's enemy. Or do you think it's without reason the Scripture says that the Spirit He has caused to live in us yearns jealously?*
> JAMES 4:1-5, HCSB

James identified the church as an adulterous church. This was a church which had become a friend of the world as opposed to a friend of the Word of God. Hostility, jealously, division, and a host of other unwholesome issues surfaced in the life of the church. But despite the condition of the church, James continued to encourage the church. He reminded them of the greatness of God's grace. He told them that "God gives greater grace." What is greater grace? It is grace that is greater than all our needs. Greater grace has no limits. It is not earth bound. Greater grace is all of the holiness of God in the persons of Jesus Christ. When we become a friend of God, we immediately becomes an enemy of the devil. This is good. Why? James said, "Whoever wants to be the world's friend becomes God's enemy." James would say to us today, "Be an enemy of the devil."

What was the reward for God's people becoming a friend of the Lord Jesus Christ? It was greater grace. Greater grace produced deeper humility. It was humility that produced submission to God and resistance from the Devil. This leads to drawing closer to God on a daily basis–holiness. Holiness eradicates a critical spirit, a judgmental heart, a legalistic attitude, a double-minded lifestyle, a quarrelsome spirit, and a prideful heart. Holiness happens when there is gospel preaching. The holiness of God was what the New Testament Church Diaspora needed. They needed change. Gospel preaching is preaching for spiritual awakening which produces deep change. This deep change causes sinful and unholy things to evaporate and vanish right before your eyes.

Once this happened within the inner life of the believers in the New Testament Church Diaspora, they were able to say. "If the Lord wills, we will live and do this or that." James wanted the believers to understand the danger of living unholy lives in the house of God. James concluded by saying to those who refuse to listen to God that such people are boastful and filled with arrogance. James said, "All such boasting is evil. So, for the person who knows to do good and doesn't do it, it is a sin." Sin is missing God's standard. It is missing God's best. Preaching for spiritual awakening is an attempt to avert missing God's standard. Isaiah the Old Testament prophet was in agreement with James the elder in the New Testament Church Diaspora. Holiness was fundamental. The holiness of God helped the Old Testament major prophet Isaiah see himself. If we could only see ourselves as God sees us, our prayer life would literally leap to another level of God's grace because God is holy!

Saints, it is time to celebrate! God is holy! Did you not know that the name Isaiah means "the Lord saves" or "the Lord our Savior." There is salvation in Isaiah's name, but more than that, there is salvation in the name of Jesus! R.C. Sproul, in his book *The Holiness of God*, reminds us that God is holy and we are not! The Bible says, "There is no one righteous, not even one..." (Rom. **3:10**, NIV). "There is no one who understands, no one who seeks God" (Rom. **3:11**, NIV). "There is no one who does good, not even one" (Rom. **3:12**, NIV). But what is it that keeps us from being holy? Sin!

"For all have sinned and fall short of the glory of God" (Rom. **3:23**, NIV). What does sin produce? Death! "For the wages of sin is death, but the gift of God is eternal life in Christ Jesus our Lord" (Rom. **6:23**, NIV). How do we avoid the wages of sin–death? Confess and repent! "That if you confess with your mouth, 'Jesus is Lord,' and believe in your heart that God raised him from the dead, you will be saved" (Rom. **10:9**, NIV). Jesus said, "Repent, for the kingdom of heaven is near" (Matt. **4:17**, NIV). Jesus said, "But unless you repent, you too will all perish" (Luke **13:3**). How then are we saved from our sins? Jesus!

You see, the time must be right. Wrong time always produce wrong results. Right time always produce right results. Timing and power are collaborative. Paul said, "...when we were still powerless, Christ died for the ungodly." Here is a picture of our strength being limited and God's power through His Son being unlimited. Choice is critical. Paul wanted the Roman believers to choose God's will over against their desire. Holiness and ungodliness were the choices in Genesis chapter three. Adam and Eve chose the forbidden fruit.

Today we have the same choice–life or death. Paul continued ministering to the New Testament Church at Rome with these words, "Very rarely will anyone die for a righteous man, though for a good man someone might possibly dare to die. But God demonstrates His own love for us in this: While we were still sinners, Christ died for us." The love of Jesus was so profound that He died for all the sin, sinners, and sins of the world. He died to defeat sin–our fallen condition (i.e., our salvation from death, hell, and the grave). He died to liberate us as sinners–our human sanctification (i.e., personal holiness). He died to forgive us of our ongoing sins–our acts of sins in the human body (i.e., our wrongs done each and every day). It was at the right time. God was on time for the Church at Rome and He is on time for us today.

The Scripture said, "For God so loved the world that He gave his one and only Son, that whoever believes in Him shall not perish but have eternal life" (John 3:16, NIV). "For the wages of sin is death, but ... (Rom. 6:23a, NIV). I am not what I want to be, but... I have let God down so many times, but... I don't know what to do with my life, but... I am so lost, but... I am so confused, but... I am a total failure, but... "For the wages of sin is death, but ...the gift of God is eternal life in Christ Jesus our Lord" (Rom. 6:23, NIV).

It was at Calvary we won! The death of Jesus defeated the death of sin! Jesus died! He died, but on that third day, He got up with all power in His hands. Jesus is Alive! The WORD is Alive! Come to Jesus and Live. Holy, holy, holy! Come to Jesus...just as you are. He loves you...and He wants to bless you and set you free...and He makes you Holy unto Himself. Come to Jesus...just as you are, let Him help you...This is an invitation to salvation. Salvation means yes to the cross. Yes to the blood. Yes to becoming a new creation (2 Cor. 5:17).

We can win the lost. Ed Silvoso, as a naïve youth, embraced this reality. I am amazed at God's power when a preacher takes the gospel to heart. Silvoso believes it begins on one's knees.[15]

---

15 Ed Silvoso, *That None Should Perish: How to Reach Entire Cities for Christ Through Prayer Evangelism* (Ventura: CA: Regal, 1994), 24.

Chapter 3

The Absence of the Glory of God

And one cried to another and said: "Holy, holy, holy is the Lord of hosts; the whole earth is full of His glory!"
ISAIAH **6:3**

God provides an unusual, extraterrestrial prophetic report to capture the undivided attention of the major prophet Isaiah. Read carefully as we do our own individual wire tap of this unusual conversation that these strange and horrific living creatures have with the man of God. "And one cried to another and said: 'Holy, holy, holy is the Lord of hosts; the whole earth is full of His glory!'"

The whole earth was full of the glory of God. This was not simply a part of the earth–it was the whole earth that was literally full of the magnificence, splendor, brilliance, and the radiance of the glory of God. There was no room for anything else other than the presence of the all sufficient power of God's glory. Bitterness, anger, slander, clamor, gossip, unforgiveness, disrespect, hatred, guile, lust, lies, lunatics, legalism, and prideful ambitions had to move out of the way because of the full presence of God's glory. Everywhere Isaiah looked there was glory. He looked up into the heavenly canopy and there was glory. He looked down into the pit of abyss of a thousand times ten thousands upon thousands of midnights and there was glory. He looked eastward beyond the sphere of the rising sun–nothing but glory. He looked westward beyond the fading of the setting sun–all glory. He looked northward and cast his sight beyond the northern lights of the North Pole–glory. Then he looked deeply downward beneath the footprint of the land mass of the Antarctica as it sprawls out beyond the South Pole–glory. The glory of God was everywhere, like an impenetrable blanket of London fog looming over all of the city. There was no space for anything else other than the glory of God.

Then out of absolute silence, the *seraphs* flew over the nation of Israel and shouted. *"Holy, holy, holy is the LORD Almighty; the whole earth is full of His glory."* Qadosh! Qadosh! Qadosh! Elohim Jehovah!

If I had been there, I would have given out an African American shout and said, "Hallelujah! Hallelujah! Hallelujah! Glory! Glory! Glory! Glory Hallelujah! Glory Hallelujah! Glory! Glory! Glory! Glory! Glory! Glory! Glory! Glory! Glory! Glory! Hallelujah! Hallelujah! Hallelujah!" As a pastor, why would I do this? Because I would realize that the whole earth was full of God's glory.

The glory of God is a reflection of the Holiness of God. If that is true, then what has happened to the glory of God in the church of the Lord Jesus Christ today? What has happened to the glory of praise and worship? What has happened to the glory of spiritual excitement? What has happened to the glory of the power of the Holy Ghost? What has happened to the glory of God in the church of the Lord Jesus Christ today? The glory of God is not about God's church having *an emotional fit* or *an emotional catharsis*. Rather, it is the presence of the Spirit's power in the pews and the pulpits. That is the power of God's Holy Spirit to change lives deeply. That is deep life change. Andrew Murray, in his book *The Inner Life*, calls it the "transformation of the inner man."

Whatever Happened to the Glory of God?

Saints, we have a glory problem in the church of the Lord Jesus Christ today. There appears to be an absence of the glory of God in far too many of our churches. It is a shame that so many churches in our nation are either dead or dying. I really mean to tell you that they are literally dead or on the path to death. Some of our nation's churches in are too sick to go ahead and die, so that they can truly come to life in Christ and the power of the Spirit of God–that is the Holy Spirit. Furthermore, we have churches in our nation that are like zombies. They are the walking dead. We have churches that are religiously dead. They are shackled with formality, structure, organization, committees, business as usual, talking sessions, planning meetings, and the rest. They remain in a perpetual huddle of planning and strategizing. They are trapped in the analysis of paralysis. Evangelism is not happening. Souls are not being saved daily. Hearts are not being softened. Disciples are not being made. Yet, due to their impotent spiritual condition, they refuse to keel over and die to self, so that they can truly have life and have life more abundantly in Jesus Christ.

Is the church still effective? I have wondered: Since completing my seminary days at New Orleans Baptist Theological Seminary in 1985, I have been burdened concerning the churches in our nation. It has caused me to raise this question to numbers of ecclesiastical orders. The question is, "Why are there so many dead and dying churches in our nation?" They are dead and dying because they have lost the luster of the glory of God. Believe me, this is not a black or white problem. **This is a glory deficiency problem**. These churches in our nation are anemic. They are dead and no one has enough guts to tell them. We have a glory problem in far too many of our churches in all denominations in our nation today that are either dead or dying spiritually. Plus, we have far too many "gospel-lite" preachers in our nation, too many fearful congregants in our nation—lost people are waiting—desperately seeking someone to tell them about what it means to have new life in Jesus Christ.

A Glory Restoration Plan

We need a glory reinstatement plan to restore the glory of God in our churches today. A. W. Tozer utters these most insightful and life-changing words to those of us who are interested in seeing God's glory return. Tozer says, "What we believe about God (i.e., His glory) is the most important thing about us (i.e., our change)." In other words, we have several fundamental problems as to why God's glory has packed up its bags and moved to another place and left so many dead and dying churches in America.

A Faith Problem

Many have stopped believing in the supernatural power of God. That is a *faith* problem (Heb. **11:6**, NIV). Many just do not believe God anymore. They do not have faith in His divine Word. There is a lack of faith in His miracle working power and in the unseen, unheard, and invisible authority of God (Acts. **1:8**; Heb. **11:1**; Eph. **2:8-9**). We have a *faith* problem.

Several years ago, a little boy was told he had only 3 months to live. The little boy decided to live his life now as if he was already in heaven. So, he went out and played ball every day. He joined the cub scouts. He decided to run to school every day. He ate all the candy and cookies he could eat in a day. Then one day, his parents asked him, "Why are you doing all these strange things? Don't you know that you have been told by your doctor that you only have **3** more months to live?"

The little boy replied by saying, "Yes, I understand."

"Then why are you doing all these strange and unusual things, son? What are you doing?"

The little boy looked up toward heaven and said to his parents, "I'm only practicing. I'm getting in shape for glory. Because in just a few more months I will be running, jumping, eating, and having fun with God in heaven, in the presence of the glory of God, and I just wanted to see how it feels having fun down here now, so when I get to heaven it won't be that strange to me when I experience the magnitude of the glory of God in the presence of Jesus Christ, God's only begotten Son."

Like the little hopeful boy, Isaiah possessed a faith in God that embraced the glory of God beyond measure. This caused Isaiah to decide to join God's team in order to experience the magnitude of the glory of God, and that is why Isaiah said to God. "Here am I, send me. I'll go. In other words, I'll do whatever you want me to do God–for your glory, honor, and praise."

I wish I could have witnessed Isaiah's encounter with the glory of God. I would loved to have seen what Isaiah saw and the hopeful little boy anticipated seeing. It is not only a blessing to experience the glory of God, but it is also fun to be in the presence of Jesus. Do you notice anyone having fun down here on earth as a Christian? Are you excited about being in the house of God today? Are you fired up about the glory of God? Or are you waiting until you get to heaven before you can crack a smile?

Unfortunately, some Christians are so placid and frozen until their faces would shatter if they cracked a smile. It is a shame to have to go to church with so many unhappy, negative, joyless, dead-spirited Christians. In Mississippi, we call these types of people, members of the First Baptist Church of Lemons, Limes, Sour Grapes, and Green Persimmons.

What would we need in our churches to actually taste God's glory? What would need to happen? What kind of changes would be needed in our nation? Saints, we need the glory of God to come down right now, so that we can worship and praise God's holy and righteous name. Glory! Glory! Glory! Glory Hallelujah! The whole earth is full of God's glory.

A Finance Problem

Another reason why we have so many dead and dying churches in America is because of a *finance* problem. We don't give. Some of the cheapest people I know are the ones that count God's money at church every Sunday. Some of the tightest people I know love to be on the finance committee, but they would not even give Jesus a raise even if He performed a miracle each and every Sunday in the house of God (Matt. 23).

When I was the pastor of my first church in Petal, Mississippi, I had a deacon who was a math whiz, but he would not pay his tithes. I asked him why and he told me that paying tithes was Old Testament law and he was now living under grace. So, I agreed with him, and then I asked him, because you are now living under grace, then why don't you do what Jesus did. He gave everything he had to save the world, John 3:16.

The problem with that deacon was not law or grace. His problem was hell or heaven. He was not saved.

When Jesus saves you from your sins, you can't give Him enough. You can't do enough. You can't serve enough. You can't love enough. You can't work enough for him. Why? Jesus is Lord.

I have learned not to beg people who are spiritually dead to do what only spiritually living people can do. Don't ever ask a person who does not enjoy serving to serve because they won't serve joyfully. Do not ever ask a lady who does not cook to cook. Since she does not like cooking; you may not live to tell about it. You should always ask those who serve to serve and those who cook to cook.

Are you a giver or a taker? Do you have a *finance* problem? Do you have a problem in giving to God's house and the work of His ministry? There is a good possibility that if a person does, then he or she may be dead or dying.

Alive people love to give! Alive people love to help! Alive people love to serve! Alive people are excited about God's work. Alive people enjoy giving God the glory He deserves.

Glory! Glory! Glory! Glory Hallelujah! Hallelujah! The whole earth was full of God's glory.

A Father Problem

Finally, there is a reason why so many dead and dying churches in America exist; they have a *father* problem. God is not their father, but Lucifer is. They are not in the family of God. They are not saved, sanctified, and filled with the Holy Spirit of God's glory.

Jesus said, in John 8:31b, "*If you abide in My word, you are My disciples indeed.*" Some of our churches in America are filled with folks who are not disciples of Christ. They are not saved. They are lost. And you cannot get a lost person to do work in the house of God. Lost people do not like Sunday school. Lost people do not like giving tithes. Lost people do not like forgiving others who have sinned against them. Lost people enjoy holding grudges. Lost people will give you a huge piece of their minds at no charge. Lost people love confusion and division in God's house.

Unfortunately, we have far too many of our churches that are populated with sinners pretending to be Saints. They are lost in the house. Just like the prodigal son's older brother who remained home–he was at home–lost. He never left the physical place of home, but he was still lost. He did not go to a far county like his little brother, but he was lost in his father's house. He was pretending to be something that he was not–saved.

One of my favorite Looney Tunes cartoons is about Sylvester, the cat. I love Sylvester, the cat. I remember during one episode that Sylvester slipped and fell and a coat of paint unknowingly went down his back. Peppy La Pew, the skunk, saw Sylvester, the cat, and he thought Sylvester, the cat, was a lady skunk. Peppy La Pew, the skunk, did everything possible to make Sylvester, the cat, his bride. Sylvester was a cat that looked like a skunk. But he was really a kitty cat.

Sometimes we as Christians look like we are unsaved. That is not good. However, what makes us different from sinners is Jesus Christ. We are saved. We know that God is holy! We desire God's glory! Glory Hallelujah! Glory! Hallelujah! The whole earth was full of God's glory.

Our souls are filled with the glory of God. Our hearts are filled with the glory of God. Our attitudes are filled with the glory of God. Our spirit is filled with the glory of God.

When the Glory of God Returns

When will the glory of God return to our nation's churches? *First*, it is when we see the Lord. Isaiah saw the Lord. He was seated on a throne, high and exalted, and the train of his robe filled the temple. The temple is a symbol of our hearts. Our hearts must see the Lord before the glory of God returns. *Second*, it is when we see ourselves. Isaiah saw himself. He saw his own sinfulness before the Lord. The glory of God will not return as long as we refuse to see how sinful and ungodly we are in the house of God. Then *third*, it is when we surrender to the lordship of Jesus Christ and begin to serve immediately. Isaiah submitted to the glory of God and said, "Here am I. Send me!" Then Isaiah got up and served the Lord willingly, reverently, and totally.

You will know when the glory of God returns in your life and in the life of the church in America when our eyes are open to see what God sees, our temples are cleaned out for God's glory, and our hands, and feet are ready to get up and get busy and do what God has told us to do. Then the glory of God will come back.

Has the glory of God departed from your family, from your life, from your job, from your finances, from you? Or are you filled with God's glory? Are you filled with His love? Are you filled with His forgiveness? Are you filled with His grace and mercy? Are you filled with His power and authority? Are you filled with the glory of God?

Or are you dead in the water? Are you empty? Would you like a refilling?

Your Personal Invitation to Experience God's Glory

First, if you would like a refilling of God's glory in your life, and you also desire our nation to be refilled with the glory of God, then get on your knees and ask Almighty God to fill our nation full with the glory of God, and you as well.

Second, some of you need to pray for dead and dying churches in our nation where the glory of God has departed. God is getting ready to write "Ichabod" over the doors of some churches. Pray for dead and dying folks in our nation, who are on the verge of having God write "Ichabod" over their life. Ask God to bring back His glory to dead and dying churches in our nation and dead and dying people in our churches.

Third, surrender your hands, feet, tongue, heart, mind, body, conversation, gifts, love, obedience, and your spirit back to God and His church. You know what you need to do.

How to Celebrate God's Glory

Jesus got up out of His seat in heaven and came down from the glory of God to restore the glory of God on earth with man and God. Jesus hung on a cross called Calvary to restore the glory of God. Jesus gave up the ghost to restore the glory of God. Jesus died to restore the glory of God. Jesus was buried in a borrowed tomb to restore the glory of God.

Then Jesus rose from the grave to restore the glory of God. Jesus restored the glory of God back to mankind when He rose from the dead. Where is the glory of God right now?" God's glory is with us right now. His glory has been restored by His death, burial, and resurrection at Calvary's cross. The glory has returned! The glory is back! Jesus is alive!

Glory! Glory! Glory! Glory Hallelujah! Glory! Hallelujah! Hallelujah! Hallelujah! The whole earth is full of God's glory.

Confess and Repent the Path to God's Glory

If while reading this you realize you do not know the Lord as personal Savior, then ponder this. Paul says, *"That if you confess with your mouth, 'Jesus is Lord,' and believe in your heart that God raised Him from the dead, you will be saved"* (Rom. **10:9**, NIV). There was no substitute for confession in the believers. This has not changed for us today. Confession of sin is needed in far too many churches in this postmodern society.

Confession void of repentance is simply words without actions. Jesus said, *"Repent, for the kingdom of heaven is near"* (Matt. **4:17**, NIV). Nearness was the location of the kingdom of heaven. God desired nearness with His people. He passionately desires nearness to all Christians today.

Confession, repentance, and nearness all work together for our good. But unless repentance occurs, we will all perish (Luke **13:3**). We will all end up separated from the presence of God and assigned to the Devil and his angels in hell. However, change through the preaching of the gospel of Jesus Christ produces life eternal. Paul declared, *"You see, at just the right time, when we were still powerless, Christ died for the ungodly. Very rarely will anyone die for a righteous man, though for a good man someone might possibly dare to die. But God demonstrates His own love for us in this: While we were still sinners, Christ died for us"* (Rom.**5:6-8**, NIV).

Christ died for all of us. He died for the world. Why would He died for the world? Christ so loved the world. John reports the words of our Savior and Lord, *"For God so loved the world that He gave His one and only Son, that whoever believes in Him shall not perish but have eternal life"* (John **3:16**, NIV). *"For the wages of sin is death, but ...* (Rom. **6:23**a, NIV). Spiritual death is the death of a man's soul. The absence of the glory of God is a picture of spiritual death to the soul.

Chapter 4

Blow Your Trumpet

So Gideon and the hundred men who were with him came to the out-post of the camp at the beginning of the middle watch, just as they had posted the watch; and they blew the trumpets and broke the pitchers that were in their hands.

JUDGES **7:19**

The Wisdom of God

What would you do if the Chairman of Deacons raised his hand in one of your Bible classes and said, "Pastor, stop teaching the Bible as if you think that it is truly the Word of God. I am an astrophysicist with my PhD from Howard University and have earned three graduate degrees from Harvard, Princeton, and Yale. In addition to this, I have studied in England, South Africa, Japan, Egypt, and Jerusalem. Pastor, you are crazy! The Bible is just another book. It is not the Word of God. And you need to stop lying to these innocent and ignorant people, as if you think that you know for a fact that this old, dusty, outdated book is indeed the Word of God!" What would you say? I know what I would say personally to the "ex-chairman of the deacons' ministry" of that congregation. But what would you say to such an intelligent and powerful man? I would have to "Blow My Trumpet."

> *For the message of the cross is foolishness to those who are perishing, but to us who are being saved it is the power of God. For it is written: "I will destroy the wisdom of the wise, And bring to nothing the under-standing of the prudent."*
>
> *Where is the wise? Where is the scribe? Where is the disputer of this age? Has not God made foolish the wisdom of this world? For since, in the wisdom of God, the world through wisdom did not know God, it pleased God through the foolishness of the message preached to save*

those who believe. For Jews request a sign, and Greeks seek after wisdom; but we preach Christ crucified, to the Jews a stumbling block and to the Greeks foolishness, but to those who are called, both Jews and Greeks, Christ the power of God and the wisdom of God. Because the foolishness of God is wiser than men, and the weakness of God is stronger than men.

1 CORINTHIANS 1:18-25

The Bible Is God's Word: It's In the Book

Would you not agree that the Bible is the Word of God? Would you not agree that when the Bible speaks, there is an end of all controversy? Would you agree that when there is a conflict between what the Bible says and what men say, we must take our stand with Peter, and say, "We ought to obey God rather than men"? You are *The Trumpeters of God.* God's Word is without a doubt the all-sufficient rule of faith and practice. The Bible is a spiritual book and cannot be interpreted as other books. Since the Holy Spirit inspired it, so the Holy Spirit must reveal its truth to the minds and hearts of men. When illuminated by the Spirit of God, the Bible is sufficient in its message. There is no need for further revelation. The Bible tells us all we need to know about the past, the present, and the future.

The Bible is the divinely inspired Word of God. "All Scripture is God-breathed" (2 Tim. 3:16, NIV). It is, therefore, our one sufficient and authoritative rule of faith and practice. The Bible does not contain the *words* of God–it is the written Word of God! No one part of the Bible is more inspired than any other. The Bible was not conceived in the minds of man but in the heart of God. Peter tells us how the Scriptures came: "...men spoke from God as they were carried along by the Holy Spirit" (2 Pet. 1:21, NIV). The Scriptures were written by men, but those men were inspired by God–were moved by the Holy Spirit for their task. The Bible is *true* and the Bible is *truth*. All 66 sacred books have been given to us by God to lead, guide, and direct the total affairs of the church, community, family, marriage, and home. Thank God that we have a Word from God.

For the word of God is living and active. Sharper than any double-edged sword, it penetrates even to dividing soul and spirit, joints and marrow; it judges the thoughts and attitudes of the heart.

HEBREWS 4:12, NIV

Who Are We? Encouragers, Educators, Equippers, and Edifiers

The Reverend Dr. John T. Smith, Sr., made a great statement: "Gospel preachers and pastors should be helping and inspiring each other to strive for excellence and effectiveness in all areas of ministry." Then he continued by outlining four distinct values.

1. The value of encouragement
2. The value of education
3. The value of equipping
4. The value of edification

Concerning the value of education, he said, "We believe that pastors and ministers should be exposed to and equipped with new tools and knowledge in ministry that will help them fulfill their calling more effectively, efficiently, and in a relevant manner. In this way, we can truly make a difference in the churches where God has assigned us to serve."

Though education may be necessary, we need the wisdom of God to know how to use the knowledge gained from education. Education without God's wisdom is foolish. Psalm 14:1 states, "The fool has said in his heart that there is no God." That is why all education needs divine revelation, spiritual inspiration, and profound illumination with profuse perspiration! This is what we call gospel preaching! So, "Blow Your Trumpet!" The apostle Paul declared:

I am not ashamed of the gospel, because it is the power of God for the salvation of everyone who believes: first for the Jew, then for the Gentile. For in the gospel a righteousness from God is revealed, a righteousness that is by faith from first to last, just as it is written: "The righteous will live by faith."
ROMANS 1:16-17

Blow Your Trumpet!

Allow me one more illustration to help us "Blow Our Trumpets" with a little more effectiveness and ease. I heard another pastor speak from Judges 7, dealing with the story of Gideon. He encouraged us to "blow our trumpets" in such a way that the Midianites are run out of our town. In Judges 7:19b (NIV) the Bible says, "They blew their trumpets and broke the jars that were in their hands." After this the Midianites got out of town!

Much sin is in the camp in our day and it needs to be run out of town. For example, teen pregnancy is a constantly growing problem that affects teenagers both in and outside the church. How bad is the problem? According to the *National Campaign to Prevent Teen Pregnancy*'s "FACTS and STATS Report," dated August 2001, the United States has the highest rates of teen pregnancy and births in the western industrialized world. Teen pregnancy costs the United States at least seven billion annually. Nearly four in ten young women become pregnant at least once before they reach the age of 20–nearly one million a year. Eight in ten of these pregnancies are unintended and 79 percent are unmarried teens.

The rate of both hispanics and blacks, however, remain higher than for other groups. Hispanic teens now have the highest teenage birth rates. Most teenagers giving birth before 1980 were married, whereas most teens giving birth today are unmarried.

Furthermore, teen mothers are less likely to complete high school (only one-third receive a high school diploma) and are more likely to end up on welfare (nearly 80 percent of unmarried teen mothers end up on welfare). The children of teenage mothers have lower birth weights, are more likely to perform poorly in school, and are at greater risk of abuse and neglect. The sons of teen mothers are 13 percent more likely to end up in prison while teen daughters are 22 percent more likely to become teen mothers themselves.

We must confess that we have too many Midianites in our town! The dynamic of deception suggests to us that the Midianites are still in our town in the form of deceptive community support. Guess where this wonderful support is located? It is located in the labor and delivery rooms of mothers both young and old. *Planned Parenthood* desires to rob us of our kids, according to the "Keeping It Real Religious Organization." We have many Midianites in our town. Therefore, we must examine the agreements of this horrific reality.

The Power of God's Word

There was a deceptive spirit that sought to lead about 300 African Amerian pastors and churches to allow *Planned Parenthood* to come in and set up shop for the purpose of helping young boys and girls to engage in free sexuality. The concept used to try and convince these leaders was that black kids could not control themselves. The speakers came to our minister's union to present their case. The pastors all accepted the presentation. I happened to be there that day. I refuted the speakers claim from the floor. Then I requested to give a rebuttle.

Permission for the rebuttle was granted within a week. Mr. David R. Brown, Jr., *Responsible Choice Grassroots Organizer of Community Parenthood of the St. Louis Region,* came to my office on November 19, 2001, at 11:30 a.m. The purpose of his meeting was to educate me on the purpose and good-willed philosophy of *Community Parenthood and The Religious Coalition for Reproductive Choice.* Mr. Brown gave me an article titled, "Is the Fetus a Person? The Bible's View" by Dr. Robb Death Wish, who is a professor of religion and affiliate in women's studies at Miami University, Oxford, Ohio. Dr. Wish concludes that, according to his understanding of Hebrew, Aramaic, Greek, and English, the fetus is not a person. In his own reason, he concluded this to be so based on his personal assessment of the Hebrew word *nephesh.*

I challenged him directly from the Hebrew Bible and read the Scripture to him in Hebrew. While I read my Hebrew Bible, he looked at the Hebrew and said, "What's this?" Then I asked if he had ever seen this or if he could read this. He said, "No Pastor Loggins, this is strange to me." Then I proceeded to read it to him and explain to him his error.

When I gave the rebuttal, he was present. The Lord helped me to make my point by reading the literal text to the brothers and over 290 pastors and churches decided not to use the program. A few did, but eventually dropped the program from the the church. A number of pastors and leaders thanked me for my effort and said, "We knew something was wrong, but we just could not place our finger on it."

I simply wanted to help pastors see how evil and deceptive the evil one is. Praise God we were able to "kick that spirit out of St. Louis!" They packed their bags and got out of town.

Dr. Wish needed to read his Hebrew Bible again. In Genesis **2:7**, in *Biblia Hebraica Stuttgartensis*–The Hebrew Bible–a first-year Bible student knows that to interpret the Bible correctly you must apply the *General Principles of Interpretation* to achieve basic *Biblical Hermeneutical Balance.* One of the general principles of hermeneutics is *context.* So, from an elementary perspective, Dr. Wish made an "F" on *context.*

The question he was trying to address was "Is the Fetus a Person?" A first-year Bible student would have said, "Yes, indeed." Genesis **2:7** reads from the literal Hebrew like this, "And became the man a soul living" (literal translation). "And man became a living soul" (KJV). Dr. Ward failed to do what a first-year Bible student does, that is, simply read the Bible the way it is written. As a matter of fact, he even failed to follow the rules of simple English grammar. He did not finish a basic phrase. Therefore, in so doing, he inappropriately lifted *nephesh* out of context and dropped the *hayah*, leaving him to say that the man was a *nephesh*. But a first-year Bible student would correct him by saying, man is not a *soul*, but a *living* soul.

Truth is not based upon human understanding, but upon the supernatural wisdom of God's eternal power and the Holy Spirit's counsel. "But the Counselor, the Holy Spirit, whom the Father will send in My name, will teach you all things and will remind you of everything I have said to you" (John **14:26**, NIV).

The Practicality of God's Word

The world argues that we must *keep it real*, if we are going to save our children. But whose standard are we going to use to help us *keep it real*? Who will determine the true definition of what is in essence real?

The Reverend D. Major Fake, Christian educator and Pastor of The Reunion Baptist Church in Washington, DC, for *The Black Church Initiative of the Religious Coalition for Reproductive Choice*, has suggested how spiritual leaders in our community could *keep it real*.

The Scripture never told us to *keep it real*. However, God did tell us to "Be holy, because He is holy." One can be *real* without being holy. But one cannot be holy without being *real*. Holiness is not simply *keeping it real*. Holiness is keeping it true. "Then you will know the truth, and the truth will set you free" (John **8:32**, NIV).

As "Trumpeters of God" if we would simply "Blow Our Trumpets" a little louder and a little longer, God will give us the city and the Midianites will have to pack up their bags and get out of town.

It is time for us to do more than just *keep it real*! The time has come for us to "be holy as He is holy." Why? Because that's what the Word of God says. The Bible says, "Thy word is a lamp to my feet and a light for my path." "Thy word, O Lord, is eternal." The Bible says, "We are to live according to the Word of God." The Psalmist declared, "I have hidden Thy Word in my heart that I might not sin against God." In **2** Timothy **4**, the Bible says:

In the presence of God and of Christ Jesus, who will judge the living and the dead, and in view of His appearing and His kingdom, I give you this charge: Preach the Word; be prepared in season and out of season; correct, rebuke and encourage–with great patience and careful instruction. For the time will come when men will not put up with sound doctrine. Instead, to suit their own desires, they will gather around them a great number of teachers to say what their itching ears want to hear. They will turn their ears away from the truth and turn aside to myths. But you, keep your head in all situations, endure hardship, do the work of an evangelist, discharge all the duties of your ministry.

2 TIMOTHY **4:1-5**, NIV

Jesus said to the Devil in Matthew **4:4**, "It is written, 'Man shall not live by bread alone, but by every word that proceeds from the mouth of God.'" Satan, the Father of Lies said that physical bread *is what man needs.* Jesus wanted to give us bread and the Word of God. This kind of spiritual bread is what our teens need, the church needs, a homosexual needs, prostitutes need, casino gamblers need, what liars need, what women, men, children, schools, governments, educators, scholars, millionaires, billionaires, bill collectors, and people in debt, people out of debt, sinners and saints alike need.

Jesus was making it clear that man's real need is related to the amount of spiritual bread–God's Word–he has been digesting. One might say, "We may be eating a lot of bread, but we are not digesting it." Undigested bread will cause a white man to become a racist. Undigested bread will cause a black man to hate a white man. Undigested bread will cause a man to sleep with another man and still be called a pastor, preacher, an evangelist, teacher, priest, or even a minister of music in God's church. Undigested bread will cause a Christian to lie on his/her taxes. Undigested bread will cause deacons not to deak! Undigested bread will cause a trustee to become untrustworthy! Undigested bread will cause a choir to cut up. Undigested bread will cause religious leaders to join hands with the Midianites (*Planned Parenthood*) to save our kids. [Bread of Heaven! Bread of Heaven! Feed me 'til I want no more.]

Therefore, Jesus said to the Devil, "Man does not live on bread alone, but on every word that comes from the mouth of God." Let God fix our problems. What we really need to *keep it real* is to see the Lord. Isaiah said,

In the year that King Uzziah died, I saw the Lord sitting on a throne, high and lifted up, and the train of His robe filled the temple. Above it stood seraphim; each one had six wings: with two he covered his face, with two he covered his feet, and with two he flew. And one cried to another and said: "Holy, holy, holy is the Lord of hosts; The whole earth is full of His glory!" And the posts of the door were shaken by the voice of him who cried out, and the house was filled with smoke.

So I said: "Woe is me, for I am undone! Because I am a man of unclean lips, And I dwell in the midst of a people of unclean lips; For my eyes have seen the King, The Lord of hosts."

Then one of the seraphim flew to me, having in his hand a live coal which he had taken with the tongs from the altar. And he touched my mouth with it, and said: "Behold, this has touched your lips; Your iniquity is taken away, And your sin purged."

Also I heard the voice of the Lord, saying: "Whom shall I send, And who will go for Us?" Then I said, "Here am I! Send me."

ISAIAH **6:1-8**

All of us have a *lip* problem. We all have unclean lips. We need the Word of God to change our community in a way in which the world cannot. Midianites are in essence undigested bread eaters.

I believe that the only way we are going to help our children *keep it real* is when we keep it real and confess our sins as leaders, pastors, ministers, teachers, Christians, and the people of God before God and man. This means we need revival in our churches. What is a revival? **A revival is when we as Christians live the way that God has instructed us to live in accordance with His Word.**

Malachi addresses several issues inherent in the ministry of the priest. God placed the priest in charge of leading the people to Himself. The priests were not on their job. Hearing God was not on their agenda. The heart of God was not their concern. The Lord said, "If you will not hear, and if you will not take it to heart, to give glory to My name..." The Lord of hosts said, "I will send a curse upon you and I will curse your blessings." The blessings of the Lord were supposed to come through the ministry of the priest. They had a simple job. Their job was to blow their trumpets of righteousness and cleanliness. They were God's representatives before the people. However, because of their disobedience the Lord declared that He would curse them, rebuke them, and spread offal on their faces. God had grown sick and tired of the pathetic leadership demonstrated by the priests.

The priests had failed. How could they lead the Lord's people in being obedient to His commandments yet they were blatantly disobedient and disrespectful to the sacred things of God. Hearing and obeying the instructions of the Lord was the last thing on their minds. Instead of seeking God first, they sought to please their own selfish desires and passions. "Seek ye first the kingdom of God and His righteousness and all these things will be added unto you" (Matt. **6:33**). God was clearly last and not first in the life of His priests.

The priests were guilty of breaking the commandments of God. Even by breaking one commandment, they were guilty of breaking them all. The Lord's heart was grieved. The Lord said, "For the lips of the priest should keep knowledge, and people should seek the law from his mouth; for he (the priest) is the messenger of the Lord of hosts." As the Lord's representative the priests failed. They departed from the way of the Lord resulting in many people stumbling along with them over the law of God. In the eyes of God, they were corrupt. The Lord said that the priests have corrupted the covenant of Levi. God charged the priests with contempt of court. He overruled them from the highest priests to the lowest priests. Showing partiality in handling the sacred things of God were the actions of the priests.

> [The priests failed the Lord.] *"And now, O priests, this commandment is for you. If you will not hear, and if you will not take it to heart, to give glory to My name," Says the Lord of hosts, "I will send a curse upon you, and I will curse your blessings. Yes, I have cursed them already, because you do not take it to heart.*
>
> [The priests mishandled the Lord's work.] *Behold, I will rebuke your descendants and spread refuse on your faces, the refuse of your solemn feasts; and one will take you away with it. Then you shall know that I have sent this commandment to you, That My covenant with Levi may continue," Says the Lord of hosts. "My covenant was with him, one of life and peace, and I gave them to him that he might fear Me; so he feared Me and was reverent before My name.*
>
> [The priests possessed lying lips.] *The law of truth was in his mouth, and injustice was not found on his lips. He walked with Me in peace and equity, and turned many away from iniquity. For the lips of a priest should keep knowledge, and people should seek the law from his mouth; for he is the messenger of the Lord of hosts.*
>
> [The priests corrupted the covenant of Levi.] *But you have departed from the way; you have caused many to stumble at the law. You have corrupted the covenant of Levi," Says the Lord of hosts. "Therefore I also have made you contemptible and base before all the people, because you have not kept My ways but have shown partiality in the law."*
>
> MALACHI **2:1-9**

Brothers, it's time for us to Blow Our Trumpets! God wants us to blow until we run all the Midianites out of our town! So, Brothers, Blow Your Trumpet! Blow Your Trumpet! Blow Your Trumpet!

A Call to Personal Holiness: Blow Your Trumpet!

Since the Bible is indeed the Word of God, then God's Word is true. "Be holy, because I am holy." We need to "Blow Our Trumpets" of Holiness. Why? Because God is holy. But what does a holy life look like today?

First, look at the unholy life–the acts of the sinful nature.

Now the works of the flesh are evident, which are: adultery, fornication, uncleanness, lewdness, idolatry, sorcery, hatred, contentions, jealousies, outbursts of wrath, selfish ambitions, dissensions, heresies, envy, murders, drunkenness, revelries, and the like; of which I tell you beforehand, just as I also told you in time past, that those who practice such things will not inherit the kingdom of God.
GALATIANS **5:19-21**

Second, look at the holy life–the fruit of the Spirit.

But the fruit of the Spirit is love, joy, peace, longsuffering, kindness, goodness, faithfulness, gentleness, self-control. Against such there is no law. And those who are Christ's have crucified the flesh with its passions and desires. If we live in the Spirit, let us also walk in the Spirit."
GALATIANS **5:22-25**

We need to adopt what I call the Gideon model. It is time to "Blow Our Trumpets" of Holiness all over our cities, until Jesus returns. Why? Because

Surely He has borne our griefs and carried our sorrows; yet we esteemed Him stricken, smitten y God, and afflicted. But He was wounded for our transgressions, He was bruised for our iniquities; the chastisement for our peace was upon Him, and by His stripes we are healed.
ISAIAH **53:4-5**

But He got up with all power in His hands! The Bible states,

So Gideon and the hundred men who were with him came to the outpost of the camp at the beginning of the middle watch, just as they had posted the watch; and they blew the trumpets and broke the pitchers that were in their hands.
JUDGES **7:19**

Chapter 5

Bring It All: It Is a Matter of the Heart

Bring all the tithes into the storehouse, that there may be food in My house, and try Me now in this," says the Lord of hosts...
MALACHI **3:10**

When Will God Send Revival?

How much is enough for God? How much does God want from us? Malachi Chapter **3** gives us the clear, simplistic, basic Bible study, Sunday school answer. The answer is so plain that even a preschooler in diapers can understand. That is–how much does God want from you and me? In Malachi, God says,

"Yet from the days of your fathers you have gone away from My ordinances and have not kept them. Return to Me, and I will return to you," says the Lord of hosts. "But you said, 'In what way shall we return?' Will a man rob God? Yet you have robbed Me! But you say, 'In what way have we robbed You?' In tithes and offerings. You are cursed with a curse, for you have robbed Me, even this whole nation. Bring all the tithes into the storehouse, that there may be food in My house, and try Me now in this," says the Lord of hosts, "If I will not open for you the windows of heaven and pour out for you such blessing that there will not be room enough to receive it. And I will rebuke the devourer for your sakes, so that he will not destroy the fruit of your ground, nor shall the vine fail to bear fruit for you in the field," says the Lord of hosts; and all nations will call you blessed, for you will be a delightful land," says the Lord of hosts. "Your words have been harsh against Me," says the Lord, "Yet you say, 'What have we spoken against You?' You have said, 'It is useless to serve God; What profit is it that we have kept His ordinance, and that we have walked as mourners before the Lord of hosts? So now we call the proud blessed, for those who do wickedness

are raised up; They even tempt God and go free.'" Then those who feared the Lord spoke to one another, and the Lord listened and heard them; so a book of remembrance was written before Him for those who fear the Lord and who meditate on His name. "They shall be Mine," says the Lord of hosts, "On the day that I make them My jewels. And I will spare them as a man spares his own son who serves him." Then you shall again discern between the righteous and the wicked, between one who serves God and one who does not serve Him."

MALACHI **3:7-18**

God wants to bless His churches in such a way that it would literally blow our missilogical mindset for the sake of the Kingdom of God. So, I believe God wants to elevate our blessed assurances. However, this remains a human impossibility and an effective tragedy, as we continue to sit on premises, while we continue to sing "Standing on His Promises" and do what it is right according to God's Word, to God's Will, to God's Work, and to God's Way! The time has come for us to give from the overflow of our hearts and not from the bottom of the barrels of our heads. The time has come for each of us to "Bring It All to the Lord!" But we will never "Bring It All to the Lord" unless our hearts are right with God.

God's Favor Requires Change

God's people wanted to know how to regain God's favor without having a heart change. Averting the oncoming punishment that was just around the bend was their major concern. God said to His people, Israel, your solution: "Is to return to Me…" Nothing will be right in the people of God until their heart is right! Until their heart was right, God would not bless them and would not remove His coming judgment. God's righteous indignation toward unconfessed sins and unrepentant hearts would be removed if the people of God will do this: "Return to Me and I will return to you."

In Matthew **6:33**, Jesus said, "But seek first the kingdom of God and His righteousness, and all these things shall be added to you." God must be first! Isaiah **55:6** says, "Seek the Lord while He may be found, call upon Him while He is near." Saints, there are times when God is so near that is seems we can almost touch Him. His closeness brings comfort like being wrapped in a warm baby blanket in the middle of the night.

While visiting people at the hospital one day, I met a man in the bed next to the person I had gone to see. He was shivering like a leaf on a tree in the dead of winter. He got on the phone and called his nurse and pleaded for a warm blanket. The nurse came in the nick of time and wrapped him, like a little baby boy, in several warm blankets; when she finished, the grown man said, "Aaaaah…"

God wants to wrap each of us in His warm blanket of grace and mercy so that our cold hearts will melt to do our Master's will. Then we cannot just *have* church but *be* the church!

God's people acted as if they had no idea what God was talking about in Malachi 3:7. They said to God, "God: 'How are we to return?" Others may state it this way, "God, we just don't understand. We don't know what you are talking about. God, what do you mean? Can you explain it to us in plain English?" God answered, "Will a man rob God? Yet you have robbed me." Then the people of God complicated the problem even more: The people of God said: "In what way have we robbed You?" In other words, God what did we do so wrong? We don't understand. Then God said, let me make it plain, this is what you have done. You have robbed me "In tithes and offerings…" Then God says: "You are cursed with a curse, for you have robbed Me, even this whole nation." Why? "Because you are robbing Me."

In other words, they were robbing God without a gun. They were not stealing from God. They did not do it behind God's back, that's stealing. But they were robbing God. To rob God is to do it right in God's face.

Each time we do not pay our tithes and offerings to God in His house, we are pulling out a gun and robbing Him. Some of us use a shotgun to rob God. Some of us use a .45 to rob God, while others of us use a .22 or even a pocket knife to rob God. It is as though we say, "Stick 'em up, God, you are under arrest." In Psalm 14:1, the Psalmist says from the Psalter, "The fool has said in his heart, 'There is no God.'" Then the Proverbial writer says, in Proverbs 24:7, "Wisdom is too lofty for a fool; He does not open his mouth in the gate."

God ought to be like E. F. Hutton to us. When He speaks, we ought to obey. My mother was just like E.F. Hutton. When she spoke, you simply obeyed. We need to do what the Lord commands.

God commanded us to make disciples of all nations. Jesus said:

> *Go therefore and make disciples of all the nations, baptizing them in the name of the Father and of the Son and of the Holy Spirit, teaching them to observe all things that I have commanded you; and lo, I am with you always, even to the end of the age. Amen.*
> MATTHEW 28:19-20

Saints, it's time for us to get with God's program and make disciples, not just church members. It is time for us to *go to work*! I left a good old-fashioned Baptist fighting meeting a few days ago. While I was on my way home, I saw two Mormons walking the streets making more Mormons, while we were in an old-fashioned Baptist fighting meeting. We need to stop fighting and go to work!

Malachi **3:10** gives the solution to the problem—bring it all to the Lord! If we would bring it all we would see God bring His blessings.

Three Promises

The obedience of God's people brings three promises:

1. The Promise of Prosperity, Malachi **3:10**b.
2. The Promise of Protection, Malachi **3:11**.
3. The Promise of a Place, Malachi **3:12**.

1. The Promise of Prosperity—The people of God had been suffering for many years. Frankly, they did not know where to turn because of entrenched disobedience. Israel's heart had grown cold and the pleasures of sin had replaced the power of the proclamation of God's commandments.

Sin in the life of God's people created confusion and conflict in their hearts. Israel did not obey God, living as if God's instructions were only suggestions. The nation's testimony was a false testimony to the pagan tribes of that day.

However, God was still faithful and true. He loved Israel despite their entrenched disobedience and complacent hearts of arrogance and evil. Malachi reports hope in the midst of a hopeless situation. The prophet wanted Israel to know that change was on the way. The Lord would not allow their sins to erase them from the platform of prominence and power to change the world. That is why the Scripture reports to watch and see if God, "...will not open for you the windows of heaven and pour out for you such blessing that there will not be room enough to receive it" (Mal. **3:10**b). What a day of rejoicing that will be when our brokenness shall be overcome by blessing and benefits. How would you feel if God said He would open the windows for you? I know how I would have felt. I would have had to engage in a period of serious down-home praise.

There was a time when Baptists used to shout. I don't know what has happened. We don't shout the way we used to. Maybe the reason why we don't is that we don't think it is either necessary or appropriate. Maybe we have replaced simplicity with sophistication. My mother and my aunts did not do this. When it came to true spirituality, shouting and giving God praise were without options. This was their way to say to God, "Lord, You are worthy of all our praise. We love You, Lord. We thank You, Lord. Father, if we had ten thousands tongues, we could not give You all the praise and worship You deserve." Celebration and praise filled the house of the Lord each and every Lord's Day.

2. The Promise of Protection–The Bible says, "And I will rebuke the devourer for your sakes, so that he will not destroy the fruit of your ground, nor shall the vine fail to bear fruit for you in the field" (Mal. **3:11**).

Israel needed hope. They were on the road to 400 years of no Word from God. However, God was preparing them for His next move. Unfortunately, far too many times, we are not ready when God is ready. Tragic as this may be, it does not have to remain this way.

3. The Promise of a Place–God knows how to care for His people. Although they were disobedient, God still took care of them. His care was not predicated on works, but love. Malachi **3:12** says, "all nations will call you blessed, for you will be a delightful land." If we choose to "Bring It All"–bring the whole tithe into the storehouse of God…then we would experience a supernatural experience like the people of God in Malachi. We too can obtain all three of these promises right now!

The Promise of Prosperity is in fact biblical prosperity. Biblical prosperity has no human limitations. The mind of man is unable to fathom the heart of God when it comes to prosperity. Our promise of prosperity is available because our Father is rich. Psalm **24:1** says, "The earth is the Lord's, and all its fullness…"

The Promise of Protection is present–because we are covered by the armor of God. Paul said, "Finally, my brethren, be strong in the Lord." It was in the Lord where the people's strength resided. Residential strength is connected to renewal and protection. As we grow strong in the Lord, our heavenly Father renews us day-by-day. Daily strength produces inner power. It is the power of His might. Putting on the full armor of God is more than just words. Armoring oneself with this type of power establishes the footing of the Christian warrior. The warrior is now able to stand against the craftiness and games of the evil one–Satan.

Contrary to popular opinion spiritual warfare is real. Evil is real. The devil is real. The spirit of the unholy is alive and active in our world today. For we are not struggling with the natural, we are in a battle with the supernatural. Principalities, powers, rulers of the darkness of this age, spiritual forces of wickedness reside in extremely high places. We must remain equipped and suited up for this battle. The battle is with the world, the flesh, and the devil.

• Be Strong in the Lord

Finally, my brethren, be strong in the Lord and in the power of His might. Put on the whole armor of God, that you may be able to stand against the wiles of the devil. For we do not wrestle against flesh and blood, but against principalities, against powers, against the rulers of the darkness of this age, against spiritual hosts of wickedness in the heavenly places. Therefore take up the whole armor of God, that you may be able to withstand in the evil day, and having done all, to stand.

Our success comes when we are willing to stand. Notice carefully, Paul did not say fight, he said, "Stand." Standing implies trusting in the Lord with all our hearts, our minds, our souls, and our spirits. We are not to take on Satan himself. We are to stand and give testimony of the sufficiency of the person and power of the Lord Jesus Christ. Christ will defeat the evil one in due season.

As we are standing, we are completely suited up for battle. Remember our job is not to engage the evil one in hand-to-hand combat. Our jobs are to stand our ground on the eternal testimony of the Word of God. God's Word through the person of Christ will defeat Satan. Hebrews **4:16**, lets us know that God's Word is shaper than a two edged sword. The sword of the Spirit is the Word of God. Daily, we are to hide God's Word in our hearts.

• Stand Therefore

Stand therefore, having girded your waist with truth, having put on the breastplate of righteousness, and having shod your feet with the preparation of the gospel of peace; above all, taking the shield of faith with which you will be able to quench all the fiery darts of the wicked one. And take the helmet of salvation, and the sword of the Spirit, which is the word of God; praying always with all prayer and supplication in the Spirit, being watchful to this end with all perseverance and sup plication for all the saints–and for me, that utterance may be given to me, that I may open my mouth boldly to make known the mystery of the gospel, for which I am an ambassador in chains; that in it I may speak boldly, as I ought to speak.

EPHESIANS **6:10-20**

Finally, the Promise of a Place is revealed as Heaven being our home. Heaven is that eternal place we call home. Home is where Jesus is. Jesus is seated at the right hand side of God in heaven–home.

• The Trumpet of God

For the Lord Himself will descend from heaven with a shout, with the voice of an archangel, and with the trumpet of God. And the dead in Christ will rise first.

1 THESSALONIANS **4**:**16**

There are times I get lonely for home. I look forward someday in seeing my aunt Minnie, my mother, Mudea (that is my wife's grandmother), and a host of others. I want to see Abraham, Isaac, and Jacob. I desire to spend time with Moses, Joshua, and David. I will be able to spend precious time with Peter, James, John, Paul, Silas, and the rest of the disciples. I will be able to talk with A. W. Tozer, C. S. Lewis, Jonathan Edwards, Andrew Murray, Augustine, Martin Luther, John Calvin, John and Charles Wesley and a host of other saints of God. However, my greatest desire is to see Jesus. The same Jesus that died on Calvary's cross for you and me.

Conclusion

The WORD of LIFE, Jesus Christ, the LIVING WORD, the WORD made flesh and dwelling among us will keep us encouraged! That WORD, "...was wounded for our transgressions, He was bruised for our iniquities; the chastisement for our peace was upon Him, and by His stripes we are healed." (Isa. **53**:**5**). Jesus brought it all! Success depends on "Bringing It All!"

The songwriter *I Surrender All* said it best:

All to Jesus I surrender; all to Him I freely give; I will ever love and trust Him, in His presence daily live. Refrain: I surrender all, I surrender all, all to Thee, my blessed Savior, I surrender all. All to Jesus I surrender; humbly at His feet I bow, worldly pleasures all forsaken; take me, Jesus, take me now. All to Jesus I surrender; make me, Savior, wholly Thine; fill me with Thy love and power; truly know that Thou art mine. All to Jesus I surrender; now I feel the sacred flame. O the joy of full salvation! Glory, glory, to His name!

So, bring it all: it's a matter of the heart! So, what hinders the heart? Sin! George O. McCaleph, Jr., says one of the key sins crippling the church of the

Lord Jesus Christ is the sin of secular thinking. Dr. McCaleph writes, "...one of the greatest sin problems of the church is the abuse of this scripture."[1]

> *Trust in the Lord with all your heart, and lean not on your own understanding; In all your ways acknowledge Him, and He shall direct your paths.*
>
> PROVERBS **3:5-6**

McCaleph contends that we do not trust God. Our response should be to get our heart in line with God's Word as John said, "If we confess our sins, He is faithful and just to forgive us our sins and to cleanse us from all unrighteousness" (**1** John **1:9**). Dr. McCaleph is on target. We must learn to trust God. Trusting God means surrendering our all to Him in all things–it's a matter of our hearts.

---

1 George O. McCalep, Jr., *Sin in the House: Ten Crucial Church Problems with Cleansing Solutions* (Lithonia, GA: Orman Press, Inc., 1999), 34.

Chapter 6

Give Out of the Treasure of Your Heart

*For they all put in out of their abundance, but she out of her poverty
put in all that she had, her whole livelihood.*
MARK **12**:44

When Will God Send Revival?

Are we in need of a Spiritual Awakening? Do we need the Spirit of God
to move in our churches, in our homes, in our schools, and in our hearts?
What is it that really moves the Spirit of God when it comes to giving to God?
Mark shares the answer: "Now Jesus sat opposite the treasury and saw how the
people put money into the treasury."

Although Jesus was seated opposite the treasury His spiritual focus was
front and center on the hearts of the people. Physical position never usurps
spiritual insight. Jesus saw what others were incapable of seeing. He saw the
motives of the human soul. Earthly wealth and riches are no substitute for real
treasures. Jesus was in the right position to reposition the focus of the ones
coming to be seen of man.

The Scripture reports, "And many who were rich put in much." Much in
man's sight are mites in God's sight. Often the rich are capable of giving only
what they have–physical wealth. Physical wealth is no match for one who
gives out of the treasure of one's heart. Contrasting the rich and famous was a
poor and needy widow. When it came to her time to put what she possessed in
the offering plate, she literally gave all she had. She gave herself. "Then one
poor widow came and threw in two mites, which make a quadrans." Her coins
did not catch the attention of people. People are not impressed with small stuff.
People are often impressed with large amounts. In the eyes of man, the poor
widow's offering was a waste of time and effort. She could have stayed home.
Yet what she gave caught the heart of Christ while catching the eyes of men.

Jesus probably saw the eyes of His disciples dilated to the size of a plate. The time was perfect to teach a lesson on giving from one's heart and giving from one's hand. So, Jesus decided to call His disciples to Himself for a brief meeting. Then He said to them, "Assuredly, I say to you that this poor widow has put in more than all those who have given to the treasury; for they all put in out of their abundance, but she out of her poverty put in all that she had, her whole livelihood." More than likely the disciples were baffled. They probably said to one another, "This is impossible. How could a poor widow give more than a rich man? Jesus must be out of His mind" (Mark **12:41-44**).

However, Jesus was not. A man's heart is impossible to hide from a holy God. Disciples only saw what they could see with their eyes. Yet the eye of Christ was able to see the difference between an impoverished heart and a prosperous heart. The rich man's heart was impeded by his wealth. He was physically wealthy but spiritual impoverished. However, the poor widow's heart was an unimpeded heart. She gave out of the abundance of her heart. She gave God all she had. You can't give more, once you have given it all.

The key verses are Mark **12:43-44**. The Bible says, "So He called His disciples to Himself and said to them, 'Assuredly, I say to you that this poor widow has put in more than all those who have given to the treasury; for they all put in out of their abundance, but she out of her poverty put in all that she had, her whole livelihood.'"

Saints: **It moves God supernaturally when we humbly give out of the treasure of our hearts.**

Two Kinds of Givers

In the midst of superfluous, legalistic religiosity, Jesus lifted His disciples to a new level of spiritual understanding concerning what it means to operate at the heart level. In the Savior's teaching, His disciples would come to understand a very powerful life lesson–God always wants us to give out of the treasure of our hearts.

In this Bible passage, there are two types of people present: first–the many big-time givers and second–the one small-time giver. Jesus had His eyes on both givers. He not only saw the amount of their gifts but also the spiritual motives behind their giving.

In Mark **12:41**, the Bible says, "Now Jesus sat opposite the treasury and saw how the people put money into the treasury. And many who were rich put in much." He saw the difference in those who give from the supernatural spirit of the heart and those who give from selfish motives to be seen. The story of Ananias and Sapphira also gives insight to selfishness. Like the rich man, they cheated themselves of true riches.

The apostle Luke provided the historical account of a husband and wife team who missed God's best by their failure to give out of the abundance of their hearts. The Scripture said, "But a certain man named Ananias, with Sapphira his wife, sold a possession. And he kept back part of the proceeds, his wife also being aware of it, and brought a certain part and laid it at the apostles' feet." The Scripture said that he was a certain man. Acts recorded his name and the name of his wife. Dr. Luke also declared their true motive. Although their actions proved noble and righteous their intent was evil and deceptive.

Peter was being filled with the Holy Spirit of God on a daily basis. God was uncovering mysteries in the presence of men. Souls were not only being saved, countless numbers of people were being delivered. The church was growing by leaps and bounds. Yet, the spirit of deception remained. Peter said, "Ananias, why has Satan filled your heart to lie to the Holy Spirit and keep back part of the price of the land for yourself? While it remained, was it not your own? And after it was sold, was it not in your own control? Why have you conceived this thing in your heart? You have not lied to men but to God."

It is one thing to lie to man, it is another thing to lie to the Holy Spirit of God. Ananias and his wife both lied to God. Then Ananias heard the words of the Holy Spirit of God from the lips of Peter and he fell dead on the spot. The onlookers were petrified. The Scripture said, "Great fear came upon all those who heard these things. And the young men arose and wrapped him up, carried him out, and buried him."

Ananias was dead. His body was wrapped up and carried out of the presence of God and he was buried. This happened in a flash. "Now it was about three hours later when his wife came in, not knowing what had happened" to her husband. Peter filled with the wisdom of God and the power of the Holy Spirit of God posed a simple question. God is unlike man in many ways. For example, man most often asks deceptive questions to stump you and catch you in a lie. Whereas, God ask direct questions to liberate your soul from punishment and death in order to give you another chance.

Peter follows the pattern of the Lord and he poses a simple yet powerful question. Peter said to Sapphira, "Tell me whether you sold the land for so much?" Peter was not seeking more information; he was seeking an honest confession of sin. Sapphira was like her dead husband, she decided to lie to the Holy Spirit of God. She said, "Yes, Peter you are exactly right. I did what a good Christian woman would do. I honored the Lord with my first fruits." Sapphira lied.

Peter was probably shaking his head in disappointment and grief. He could have looked her in the eye as to say, "Sapphira tell me the truth, the whole truth and nothing but the truth." Sapphira refused to change her story. Then Peter said to Sapphira, "How is it that you have agreed together to test the Spirit of the Lord? Look, the feet of those who have buried your husband are at the door, and they will carry you out. Then immediately she fell down at his feet and breathed her last. And the young men came in and found her dead, and carrying her out, buried her by her husband."

The same lie that caused the death of her husband caused her death as well. This is one example of a husband and a wife being in complete agreement. Just because a husband and his wife are in complete agreement it does not mean they are in agreement with the Spirit of God. Some churches vote unanimously in a church business meeting and often believe God's Holy Spirit is pleased. Voting unanimously on a church issue does not make the action right in the eyes of Almighty God. Churches, like people, can be unanimously wrong. Righteous never requires a vote. Righteousness is right because it is right with God's Holy Spirit.

Despite the negative results of a husband and his wife, the Holy Spirit of God still produced a positive outcome. Great fear gripped the church of Jesus Christ. God got man's attention. People told others who were not there and the fear of the Lord spread like a wildfire in a parched forest during the dry season (Acts 5:1-11).

God wants us to give from the treasure of our hearts: Nothing more and nothing less. But how does God make His point clear? He used a woman. A woman who had three strikes against her: first—she was poor woman, second—she was a widow woman, third—she was a woman.

Jesus called attention to this woman, "But a poor widow came and put in two very small copper coins, worth only a fraction of a penny" (Mark 12:42, NIV). Now what does this mean? First—Jesus was about to show that He can use anybody. Second—with God more is less because less is more in the Master's hand.

The Apostle Paul illustrated that the power is not in the vessel (person) but in what God does with a yielded person.

But we have this treasure in earthen vessels, that the excellence of the power may be of God and not of us. We are hard-pressed on every side, yet not crushed; we are perplexed, but not in despair; persecuted, but not forsaken; struck down, but not destroyed–always carrying about in the body the dying of the Lord Jesus, that the life of Jesus also may be manifested in our body. For we who live are always delivered to death for Jesus' sake, that the life of Jesus also may be manifested in our mortal flesh. So then death is working in us, but life in you.

2 CORINTHIANS 4:7-12

Maybe some of us may have only two copper coins, but, we know that little becomes much when you place it in the Master's hand. Rubies and diamonds, silver and gold, we are children of the King wherever we go.

But how do we know that the poor widow woman gave out of the treasure of her heart? First–consider her measure–"[she]...put in all that she had." Second–consider her manner–"...she [gave] out of her poverty." Third–consider her motive–"...her whole livelihood."

"So He called His disciples to Himself and said to them, 'Assuredly, I say to you that this poor widow has put in more than all those who have given to the treasury'" (Mark 12:43). While others gave out of wealth, she gave all she had!

Jesus did that for you and me! He gave out of His poverty that we might become rich. He gave out of His suffering that we might become saved! Jesus gave everything He had. He gave all He had to live on! He gave His life so that we might have abundant life! That is why even conservative, quiet, laid-back, logical, non-emotional, mature, intellectual people ought to praise Him anyway!

Jesus died on Calvary's cross just for you and me! He died a sinner's death just for you and for me! But He did not stay dead! He got up with all power in His hands! Power to change people! Power to transform people! Power to free people! Power to heal people! Power to save people! Power! He's got the power if we would give Him the praise!

Then, one day, He's coming back! But are you ready? You do not want to wait to get ready, rather you need to be ready when He comes! That means you must prepare right now. Why?

Because there is one treasure that everyone needs! Salvation! Are you saved? Have you been born again? Do you need help? Do you need hope? Do you need a move of God in your life, in your family, in your faith, in your job?

Come to Jesus–now! Come as you are! Just come! Jesus will give you the treasure of salvation! Unfortunately, for some, pride will not let them come! Pride hinders revival! Pride hinders restoration! Pride hinders renewal! Pride hinders relationships! Pride hinders church growth! Pride hinders Christian growth! Pride is public enemy Number One! So, how do we get rid of our pride? We must empty the trash can of human pride through deep repentance so that the Lord can fill us with the treasure of salvation, sanctification, celebration, and glorification! When pride is removed, then we will not focus on our self, rather, we will give out of the treasures of our hearts!

Martin Luther gave out of the treasure of his heart, as he hung his 95 theses on the door at Wittenberg. This simple action resulted in God sending revival which changed the world! Lord: Send a revival! Lord: Send a revival! Lord: Send a revival and let it begin in my heart!…in my heart…in my heart…Lord, I want to be a Christian in my heart…in my heart…in my heart…Lord, I want to be a Christian in my heart…Lord, I want to be more loving in my heart…in my heart…Lord, I want to be more loving in my heart…in my heart…in my heart… Lord, I want to be more loving in my heart… Give out of the treasure of your heart!

Martyn-Lloyd Jones, in his masterful work titled *Revival*, provides great wisdom from the Lord:

> How Revival Comes…the first stage in revival deals with sin." Jones continues, "You see the judgment upon it. And the first sin, God's pronouncement, God's judgment upon it." And the first position, "These people who had rebelled (during the days of Moses)."[1]

God addresses sin in the house. This is His way of helping us and leading us for God's glory.

---

1 Martyn-Lloyd Jones, *Revival* (Westchester, IL: Crossway Books, 1987), 153.

Chapter 7

The Fire that Brought Change

When the day of Pentecost came, they were all together in one place. Suddenly a sound like the blowing of a violent wind came from heaven and filled the whole house where they were sitting. They saw what seemed to be tongues of fire that separated and came to rest on each of them."

ACTS **2:1-3**, NIV

Dr. Billy K. Smith, my Old Testament professor at New Orleans Baptist Theological Seminary, shared a thought provoking statement made by a Catholic bishop. This bishop stated that he observed that all of the organizational changes taking place in the institutional church today are akin to "re-shuffling the deck chairs on the Titanic!" No matter how many organizational or structural changes happen and no matter how many innovations or new techniques take place, there is no way for a church to be a church–apart from an empowering Spirit. The church of the Lord Jesus Christ will not and shall not be able to do the work of the Lord Jesus Christ apart from a power far beyond itself.

What we cannot do, God has already done. What we are planning, God has already finished. What we ponder in our limited human minds, the mind of Christ has already decided what to do, how to do it, where to do it, and to whom to do it–all at the same time. The mind of Christ is a mind that encompasses "His humility, His self-control, His servanthood, and His faith–All that is Christ."[1] Saints, we all desperately need a mind transplant. We need His mind. We need the mind of Christ.

But just what is the missing ingredient of an authentic spiritual awakening? During a weekend revival in the city of New Orleans, Dr. Smith shared this penetrating story:

---

1 T.W. Hunt and Claude King, *The Mind of Christ* (Nashville, TN: LifeWay Press, 1994), 7.

Several years ago in Africa, a missionary was told a story about a colony of monkeys that had invaded a camp. For several days, the monkeys worked (like normal human beings) without limitations, gathering firewood and methodically piling it in the center of the camp as they had seen the men do.

Day after day they continued this task of gathering all the firewood together; they all sat down around the firewood and pretended to warm themselves, knowing all the time that the wood was never put to flame. They sat there, and sat there, and sat there–freezing to death but still no fire![2]

Unfortunately, there are churches like that today. Could it be the missing ingredient in the church is fire? They have all gathered around the firewood, but there is no fire! The fire is the Holy Spirit. It is the missing ingredient in the church ordinary as opposed to the church extraordinary. Although the Holy Spirit is not there, the members continue to stack the wood even higher and higher and higher, day after day after day. But still there is no fire!

We go on programming in the church, but the fire of the Holy Spirit is not there. There is no fire!

Carl Bates said that the Holy Spirit (the ingredient that brings the fire[3] of change) could withdraw from the church, and 95 percent of our churches, and the churches would go on functioning as if He was present and then we would boast about our success due to His presence and power.

A church without the power of the Holy Spirit has misplaced priorities. A church without the power of the Holy Spirit is like a caged eagle without wings. When our priorities are wrong, we go into battle with either the wrong equipment or not enough equipment to win the war.

---

2 Paul Enns, *The Moody Handbook of Theology* (Chicago, IL: Moody Press, 1989), 278.

The basis for the filling of the Spirit is Ephesians 5:18, "be filled with the Spirit." The command to be filled with the Spirit is given in contrast to the warning "do not get drunk with wine." Drunkenness exhibits the inability of the person to control himself. The nature of the Christian's life is to be in contrast to the nature of the uncontrolled drunkard. The meaning of "filled" (Gk. *plerousthe*) is "control." The indwelling Spirit of God is the One who should continually control and dominate the life of the believer.

A further contrast can be noted between the spiritual believer and the carnal believer (1 Cor. 2:9–3:4). The carnal man is the man who lives by the power of the flesh, according to the dictates of the flesh, and the spiritual man is the man who lives by the power of the Spirit.

The "fleshly" (Gk. *sarkikos*) man is "controlled by the flesh." The solution to carnality and walking according to the old nature was to be controlled or filled by the Spirit.

3 Ibid.

So, when will this fire that brings change come to His church? What conditions are necessary for the fire to fall!

First, the people of God must be together. The Scripture says, "When the day of Pentecost came, they were all together in one place" (Acts **2:1**, NIV). Notice, "...they were all together." Don't expect God to move if we are not together. Being together is more than just simply being in the same room or the same church. Biblical togetherness has to do with the heart, not the head. If our hearts are not right with God, then it does not matter how good we are with our heads, nothing spiritual is going to happen. It is possible to experience many good activities, without the power of the Spirit. It will literally be wasted time, energy, talent, and treasure, however, without the power of God's Spirit. Biblical togetherness only comes from God's Holy Spirit when we are all together in one place. The implication is that of Paul's statement, "There is one body and one Spirit–just as you were called to one hope when you were called–one Lord, one faith, one baptism" (Eph. **4:4-5**, NIV).

Second, the people of God must be filled with heaven's agenda/strategy.[4] "Suddenly a sound like the blowing of a violent wind came from heaven and filled the whole house where they were sitting" (Acts **2:2**, NIV).

God just showed up! Nobody had to beg God to show up! Nobody had to pay God to show up! He just comes to the party because the climate is right. I was told something by a young man, who is now married. He said, "I would never go to a hot party until the time was right. That was when things were really getting hot. And usually that would not occur until about 10:00 pm." Thank God that this young man is now saved and is a very good preacher. God will not fill us up until the time is right and God will not fill us up if we are already full of something else. In order for Him to fill us up, we are going to have to empty our cups. Then, we can say, "Fill my cup Lord..."

David said it best in Psalm **23:5**, (NIV) "...my cup overflows..." God will make our cups run over–overflow! But we must first acknowledge the fact that we have empty cups that need to be filled. We can't do it on our own strength and power. We need God! The thing I like about God is this–He did not just fill one room in the house of our hearts, but the Bible says, "[He] filled the whole house where they were sitting." When God does what He does, He does it completely.

---

4 Heaven's Agenda/Strategy is "Soul Winning," that is an illustration of the Great Commission, Matt. 28:18–20.Luke 19:10 says, "For the Son of Man came to seek and to save that which was lost." The goal is to get fallen man into the presence of a faithful God. This is done through the cross at Calvary, Matt. 28:1–ff.

Third, the people must be able to see what God sees. Acts 2:3 (NIV) says, "They saw what seemed to be tongues of fire that separated and came to rest on each of them."

If we are expecting to get God-sized results, then we must possess God-sized sight. I am convinced that the reason we do not get God-sized results is that we don't have God-sized sight. The reason why we don't have God-sized sight is that we don't have God-sized faith. And don't ever forget this–**God-sized faith requires God-sized leaps of faith or God-sized challenges**. A God-sized challenge is to attempt something that, when it is accomplished, everyone will know that only God could have done it. Then the only person who would be given a pat on the back would be God! So we want to see what God sees, do a God-sized thing and then watch God show up! Are you attempting to do a God-sized thing? Something that no one else but God can help you get it done? Then I want you to know that God will send a God-sized fire to change the circumstances that we are dealing with right now!

There Was Fire...[5]

1. In the burning bush–Exodus **3:2**
2. Plagued the Egyptians–Exodus **9:23,24**
3. Led the people of Israel in the desert–Exodus **13:22**; **40:38**
4. On Mount Sinai at the giving of the law–Deuteronomy **4:11, 37**
5. Destroyed Nadab and Abihu–Leviticus **10:2**
6. Destroyed the people at Taberah–Numbers **11:1**
7. Consumed the company of Korah–Numbers **16:35**
8. Consumed the sacrifice of Gideon–Judges **6:21**
9. Consumed the sacrifice of Elijah–1 Kings **18:3**
10. Destroyed the enemies of Elijah–2 Kings **1:10,12**
11. Elijah taken up in a chariot of fire–2 Kings **2:11**

Our God is the God who answers by fire! The thing about this fire was "that it separated and came to rest on each of them." In Acts 2, this fire separated them and rested on each person present. Fire conveyed the message of the presence of the Holy Spirit of God. There was fire. Fire that burned, plagued, led, gave the law, destroyed, consumed, and taken up in a chariot of fire.

---

5 Enns, "The Holy Spirit of God is that FIRE which brings change in the hearts and souls of men."

Fourth, the people of God must be able to speak the same language (Communication). "All of them were filled with the Holy Spirit and began to speak in other tongues as the Spirit enabled them" (Acts 2:4, NIV). The Holy Spirit's fire at Pentecost in Acts 2 removed Satan's curse at Babel in Genesis 11.

The curse at Babel in Genesis 11 is the curse of confused communication. In Genesis 11, the intent of the communicator was evil. There was no good in their sight. The goal was to build a tower up to heaven and overthrow Heaven, God's throne. But God did not allow it to happen. God totally confounded or confused the language. If our plans are not God's plan, He will confuse the language. We may think that we are communicating. We may even be using the English language. But if God is not in the communication, then English is like Russian to an Italian. And things just don't get done. Why? Maybe because our hearts, motive, intent, or objective is not God's objective. But when our motive, intent, or objective is God's objective, things just happen.

Communication was happening in Acts 2. The Parthians were understanding the Medes, the Medes were understanding the Elamites, the Elamites were conversing with the residents of Mesopotamia, the residents of Mesopotamia were communicating with the Judeans, Cappadocians, people in Pontus and Asia, Phrygia and Pamphylia, Egypt and the parts of Libya near Cyrene, even visitors from Rome (both Jews and converts to Judaism); and the Cretans and Arabs were fully understanding each other. There was no static in the communication. That is the way it is when we are in the midst of the Spirit's fire. The Spirit's fire purifies the heart's intent of the people of God.

God was moving in such an incredible way, that the group of folks who were standing by on the sideline said, "What does this mean?" I could have answered their question real fast. This is what it means. The people of God were finally back together again.

God can get our generation back together again too. When that happens, people may even think that something is wrong with us because we are so together. They may even call us drunk! But that's all right, too. Because the Bible says, "Do not get drunk on wine, which leads to debauchery. Instead, be filled with the Spirit" (Eph. 5:18, NIV). When we are filled with the Spirit of God, things will get done. If we are not filled with the Spirit of God, things may get done, but they won't have any lasting power!

Recently, I watched as my neighbor changed! He became an advocate for his political candidate. Passionately, he was pushing for his political candidate throughout our neighborhood and beyond! What about us today, are we ready to change and become an advocate for our personal candidate, Jesus Christ? I am perplexed. Are we pushing for our candidate to be in office–Jesus Christ our Lord? Is the church as committed to Christ as my neighbor is to a politician? Why can't we work for free to spread the gospel of Jesus Christ and help put our candidate in office like the young man was trying to put his political candidate in office?

However, Jesus Christ, God's one and only Son[6] was so committed to us until He sent the fire that brought change–the Holy Spirit of God following His death on a cross.

Jesus Christ was so deeply committed to His Heavenly Father that He refused to come down from the cross. He died for you and me because of His commitment to our Heavenly Father. His death sent us the fire that brought change! Jesus cried out in a loud voice. "Eloi, Eloi, lama sabachthani?"–which means, "My God, my God, why have you forsaken me?" (Matt. **27:46**, NIV). Then His final words were "It is finished" (John **19:30**, NIV). And "Father, into Your hands I commit My spirit" (Luke **23:46**, NIV). I don't know about you, but that's real commitment to send us the fire that brought change. Are you ready to change?

"I'm ready for the fire of the Holy Spirit to burn a fire in my heart!" Acts **2:3** says, "They saw what seemed to be tongues of fire." So I want to know, are you ready for a change? Are you ready for God to do something new and fresh in your life? Are you ready for a mighty moving of the Holy Spirit of God in your life?

Our readiness to change falls in two categories: *membership or discipleship*. *Membership*–means being a member of the church. *Discipleship*–means you are being a disciple of the Lord Jesus Christ. My question is which one are you?

Church members are like politicians–with no fire.[7] They are not dependable. They will let us down. They are not really committed to the things of God. They will give us great lip service but no faithful service. God cannot

---

6 John 3:16–17, "The so love of God." This is *agapē*. The word *agapē* unlike *storgē*, *eros*, and *philos* conveys the message of "divine love." *Storge* is love of family. *Eros* is love of procreation or marital love. *Philos* is love of friendship (see, C. S. Lewis' book, *The Four Kinds of Love*; Affection [*storgē*], Friendship [*philos*], Eros [*eros*], and Charity [*agapē*]; also see, *Strong's Exhaustive Concordance*).

7 Enns, *The Moody Handbook Theological*, 278. "The Holy Spirit's power and presence at work in the Spiritual life of the believer produces deep change."

build His Church upon the shifting, sinking, soft, and saltless sand of church members.

But church disciples are like statesmen–with the fire that brings change. When a statesman gives us his word, we can take it to the bank and cash it. When a statesman says, go forward, there is no retreat. In other words, a disciple of the Lord Jesus Christ is like a statesman as opposed to a church member who is like a politician. A disciple or statesman is a *Mathētēs*[8]–"a learner; one who is in the process, processing and progressively growing daily in the Grace of God and the power of the Holy Spirit of God; a student; an imitator (of Jesus Christ)."[9]

Politician or Statesman

Are you a politician or a statesman? In the same way, are you a church *member* or a *disciple*? Which one are you? The fire of God will not come until you have embraced from the heart, not from the head, true discipleship. This requires progressively growing daily into a follower of Jesus Christ. In *koinē* Greek, the word for a progressive follower of Christ is a disciple.[10]

I want to give you a way to remember what a disciple is. This will be done through the identification of each character in the word disciples.

> Disciplined one, Romans **6:1-8**
>
> Imitator of Christ, Ephesians **5:1**
>
> Saved one in Christ, **2** Corinthians **5:17**
>
> Celebrative one, Psalm **100**:1-ff
>
> Insightful one, **1** Corinthians **1:18**-ff
>
> Passionate one for the lost, Romans **1:16**
>
> Love the people, John **3:16**
>
> Evangelistic one, Luke **19:10**
>
> Sacrificial one, Romans **12:1-2**

---

8 Walter A. Ewell, *The Concise Evangelical Dictionary of Theology* (Grand Rapids, MI: Baker Book House, 1991), 91.

What is a disciple? (Gk. mathetes) The characteristic name for those who gathered around Jesus during his ministry was "disciple." He was the teacher or master; they were his disciples, a term involving too much personal attachment and commitment to the rendered adequately by "pupil." In essence a disciple is one who is yet to become what he or she has the potential in becoming. In short, in the context of Christianity, a disciple is a treasured potential in the hands of the Master Carpenter, the Lord Jesus Christ.

9 2 Cor. 5:17, "...in Christ..." Eph. 5:1, "Be imitators of God..." 1 Thess. 1:6, "You became imitators of us and of the Lord..."

10 *Koinē*, *Eerdmans Dictionary of the Bible*, 532–33; 778.

Conclusion

Are you a "disciple of Jesus Christ–a faithful statesman" who has been changed and fired up! Or are you just a good church member–a good politician? The difference is *night* and *day*, or *fire* and *ice*. When we preach the Word and preach it as it is written, fire appears and the cold melts. It is time to set a fire in America. Therefore, *Preach It, Brother, Preach. Preach the Word.* When we do what the Word of God says, it will get hot. The church needs fire. And that fire is "The Fire that Brought Change."

Chapter 8
Not Too Preoccupied To Pray

"If My people, who are called by My name, will humble themselves and pray and seek My face and turn from their wicked ways, then will I hear from heaven and will forgive their sin and will heal their land."
2 CHRONICLES **7:14**, NIV

What is the church's (Ekklesia[1]) greatest need? Revival! That is, in essence, a spiritual awakening! Do you believe we need a revival in America?

Unconfessed, unrepentant sin literally is a roadblock to real revival–a revival that pierces the hearts of sinful men, while bringing them to repentance… a revival that unshackles the lost souls doomed for the pit of hell…a revival that saves souls and brings wandering souls to Jesus Christ…a revival that pleads the blood of Jesus over the unborn, unloved and underdogs…a revival that celebrates the empty tomb, that Jesus is alive…a revival that will set every church on fire with the gospel of Jesus Christ.

Do you believe that your church, pastor, deacons, mission groups, Sunday school, outreach ministries, visitation ministry, Wednesday night prayer meeting and Bible study ministries, men's groups, youth ministry, fellowship ministry, family and marriage ministry, and giving ministry…desires revival? Desiring revival suggests desiring God.[2]

---

1 *Ekklēsia*, "The common English translation of Gk. *ekklēsia*. At the time of the composition of the NT it was widely used to refer to gatherings of people in some kind of assembly. In the Greek version of the OT *ekklēsia* was used for the people of God (Israel) gathered together for an important purpose (Judg. 20:2; 1 Chr. 29:1; cf. Acts 7:38). In the NT it refers mainly to the people of God gathered in the name of Jesus or the God of Jesus Christ (Eph. 3:21; 5:23; 1 Thess.1:1; 1 Cor. 10:32). The NT understands "church" to refer to the visible expression of the gathered followers of Jesus Christ who have been grafted into a community created by God, under the banner of Jesus Christ, embodying in an anticipatory way the life and values of the new creation.

2 John Piper, *Desiring God: Meditations of a Christian Hedonist* (Sisters, OR: Multnomah Books, 1996), 25.

Is there anyone in America thirsty for the heart of God in prayer and humility? So, when will God send revival to America? In **2** Chronicles there are three prayer points in the text. First the Lord said, to Solomon, "I have heard your prayer and have chosen this place for myself as a temple for sacrifices." The Lord said, "I have heard and I have chosen." Chosen what? The Lord said, "I have chosen this place." What place? The place refers to the temple that Solomon, son of David, had built and dedicated to the Lord. Worship in the temple was the place where Israel met God. The Lord said, "I have heard your prayer and have chosen this place for myself as a temple for sacrifices." The temple was a solemn place of sacrifices to Almighty God.

Next, the Lord called Israel to genuine humility and prayer. "If my people who are called by my name, will humble themselves and pray." Humility and prayer were inextricably woven together. It is not true prayer without humility. Likewise it isn't humility devoid of prayer. It is humility and prayer. Lordship conveys both. The order was not the point. It required both, operating in harmony together, to produce revival and spiritual awakening. When the preacher preaches the gospel under the anointing of the Spirit's power, both humility and prayer operates in harmony. Preach it brother! Preach it! Preach the Word!

The final prayer point was identified as seeking the face of the Lord. Seeking the face of the Lord is critical. If one fails to turn from his or her wicked ways, nothing will be heard from heaven. Heaven's silence implies the presence of wicked hearts and prideful spirits. God heard Solomon's prayer, He called His people to humility and prayer, and He instructed them to seek His face and turn from their wicked ways.

Now read this passage prayerfully, humbly, and reverently. Read it three times. Ask the Lord to help you see what you sense God wants you see. If it requires you reading this transformational passage more than three times do it. Read it until you are able to hear the voice of the Lord. Once you have read the passage then take some time and mediate on what God said. Then you will be able to say that your eyes will be open and your ears attentive to the prayers offered in your own personal temple. Your body is the temple of the Holy Spirit. Honor God in your body. Don't ever be too preoccupied to pray.

When Solomon had finished the temple of the Lord and the royal palace, and had succeeded in carrying out all he had in mind to do in the temple of the Lord and in his own palace, the Lord appeared to him at night and said:

> *I have heard your prayer and have chosen this place for myself as a temple for sacrifices. When I shut up the heavens so that there is no*

rain, or command locusts to devour the land or send a plague among my people, if my people, who are called by my name, will humble themselves and pray and seek my face and turn from their wicked ways, then will I hear from heaven and will forgive their sin and will heal their land. Now my eyes will be open and my ears attentive to the prayers offered in this place. I have chosen and consecrated this temple so that my Name may be there forever. My eyes and my heart will always be there."

2 CHRONICLES **7:11-16**, NIV

The key verse is **2** Chronicles **7:14**a, the Lord says, "…if my people, who are called by my name, will humble themselves and pray…"

Not Too Preoccupied To Pray

Richard J. Foster, prolific author of the dynamic classic *Celebration of Discipline*, calls our attention to another one of his masterful works titled *Prayer: Finding the Heart's True Home*. In it, he boldly states that "Prayer ushers us into the Holy of Holies of God, where we bow before the deepest mysteries of the faith, and one fears to touch the Ark" of God.[3] Foster concludes by saying:

Today the heart of God is an open wound of love. He aches over our distance and preoccupation. He mourns that we do not draw near to Him. He grieves that we have forgotten Him. He weeps over our obsession with muchness and manyness. He longs for our presence.[4]

A prayerless people are a powerless people. A prayerless people are a prideful people. A prayerless people are a poor and impoverished people.

We do not pray enough. We need to find that quiet place to spend time with God. Gene Edwards calls this quiet place, "the prayer of silence."[5] I believe we need more prayer in the church. America needs prayer. We need to pray more. We don't need more money, we need more Master. We don't need a trillion-dollar stimulus package to turn our economy around; we need a bended knee and a bowed-down head, a broken and contrite spirit, pleading the blood of Jesus for the forgiveness of our sins in the Name of Jesus.

America needs prayer. Our churches need prayer. The denominations need prayer. Our pastors need prayer. Our deacons need prayer. Our music min-

---

3 Richard Foster, *Prayer: Finding the Heart's True Home* (Harper Collins: New York, 1992), XI–XII.

4 Foster, *Prayer: Finding the Heart's True Home*, 1.

5 Ibid.

istries need prayer. Our young people need prayer. Our singles need prayer. Everybody in the house of prayer needs prayer.

In other words, we don't simply need prayer in the schoolhouse; we need prayer in church house; we need prayer in the family house, but most of all we need prayer in the house of our hearts. In 1 Corinthians **6:19-20**, the Bible says, "Or do you not know that your body is the temple of the Holy Spirit who is in you, whom you have from God, and you are not your own? For you were bought at a price; therefore glorify God in your body and in your spirit, which are God's." Saints, we need prayer and Saints, we need it now! We need it because a prayerless people are a powerless people! Quiet, please. There is power in prayer. Foster esteems one of the many categories of prayer for our personal edification. He refers to it as "Simple Prayer."[6] Read closely and listen to this prayer. You will understand what is on his heart when it comes to prayer in this manner. Here it is. Are you ready? Listen prayerfully to this profound insight. Foster writes:

> What I am trying to say is that God receives us just as we are and accepts our prayers just as they are. In the same way that a small child cannot draw a bad picture, so a child of God cannot offer a bad prayer. So we are brought to the most basic, the most primary form of prayer: *Simple Prayer*. Let me describe it for you. In *Simple Prayer*, we bring ourselves before God just as we are, warts and all. Like children before a loving father, we open our hearts and make our requests. We do not try to sort things out, the good from the bad. We simply and unpretentiously share our concerns and make our petitions. We tell God, for example, how frustrated we are with the co-worker at the office or the neighbor down the street. We ask for food, favorable weather, and good health. In a sense, we are the focus of *Simple Prayer*. Our needs, our wants, our concerns dominate our prayer experience. Our prayers are shot through with plenty of pride, conceit, vanity, preciousness, haughtiness, and general all-around egocentricity. No doubt there are also magnanimity, generosity, unselfishness, and universal goodwill. We make mistakes–lots of them; we sin; we fall down; often–but each time we get up and begin again. We pray again. We seek to follow God again. And again, our insolence and self-indulgence defeat us. Never mind. We confess and begin again … and again … and again. In fact,

---

6 Ibid.

sometimes *Simple Prayer* is called the "Prayer of Beginning Again." *Simple Prayer* is the most common form of prayer in the Bible. Abraham prayed this way, as did Joseph, Joshua, Hannah, David, Gideon, Ruth, Peter, James, John, and a host of other biblical luminaries.[7]

This is *Simple Prayer*. Let us examine David's *simple prayer*.

David acknowledged his transgressions, his iniquity, and his sin. He pleaded with God to blot out his transgressions, wash him thoroughly from his iniquity, and to cleanse him from his sin. This was simplicity at its best. You can sense the spirit of humility in his prayer. David was a broken man. He was broken from within and without. As King of Israel, every tabloid, newspaper, journal, and late night show published and aired "The Life of David, King of Israel" across the media. David could have hired an image consultant to clean up his image in order to maintain his prominence and status in the Middle East. He did not. He knew what he needed. David, the King of Israel needed the Lord the King of Glory to have mercy upon him according to His lovingkindness; according to the multitude of His tender mercies. David, like the Apostle Paul, declared to the church at Rome in Romans **12:1-2**, "Therefore, I urge you, brothers, in view of God's mercy."

David had a clear view of the Lord's mercy, just as Paul had a view of God's heart for mercy toward His church. Two great men with one great and glorious view of the mercy of God. David like Paul needed change. David was on his Damascus road headed toward a heart change. Examine the parallel. Present were two great men both with two great needs and God responded to both of them with new mercy.

Sin was David's problem, but forgiveness and deliverance was the Lord's response. David had sinned and done evil in the sight of the Lord. David said, "Against You, You only, have I sinned, and done this evil in Your sight–that You may be found just when You speak, and blameless when You judge." David cried out and said, "I'm guilty in the first degree. Lord have mercy on my soul," and the Lord did.

Read David's simple prayer. As you read the prayer, ask yourself a question or two. "Have I sinned a sin like this in my life? Am I guilty of the sin of not preaching for spiritual awakening? Do I take God's Word seriously? Do I stand in need of the mercy of the Lord like King David in the Old Testament and the Apostle Paul in the New Testament? Read it here:

---

7 Ibid, 9-10.

Have mercy upon me, O God, according to Your lovingkindness; according to the multitude of Your tender mercies, blot out my transgressions. Wash me thoroughly from my iniquity, and cleanse me from my sin. For I acknowledge my transgressions, and my sin is always before me. Against You, You only, have I sinned, and done this evil in Your sight—that You may be found just when You speak, and blameless when You judge.

PSALM **51:1-4**

King Solomon, King David's Son

David got right with God. He prayed a simple prayer. He prayed a prayer of confession and repentance of sin. Like his father, King Solomon was a man of prayer as well. He prayed with power, purpose, and passion. He prayed a life-changing, earth-shattering prayer that the Lord heard. King Solomon, like his father David, was a man of *Simple Prayer*.

Entering into the presence of God, Solomon's prayer is a powerful picture and a sermon in itself. Words are impotent to communicate the depth of what is pressing on the heart of the Almighty. Solomon did not simply pray. Solomon finished his prayer. I am concerned as a preacher of the gospel of Jesus Christ that we are not finishing our prayers. Instead of praying through with simple prayers, we stop right before the Lord's response. I believe that throne room of God is littered with scores of unfinished prayers. The Holy Spirit of God probably has been saying to us, "You quit too soon. Your prayer are incomplete."

King Solomon finished his prayer. The Lord affirmed the prayer of Solomon with fire coming down from the throne room of God. His prayer was a consuming prayer. The Lord said, "Yes and the fire from heaven consumed the burnt offering and the sacrifices; and the glory of the Lord filled the temple." The Lord showed up with power and authority because Solomon finished his prayer. However, a finished prayer is by no means a way to manipulate the will of God. The Lord commands us to prayer. Our responsibility is to pray and keep on praying. The Lord's responsibility is to respond according to His will and His timing. Solomon finished his prayer and the Lord answered with fire from heaven.

Prayerfully, read and meditate on the simple prayer of David's son, Solomon, and compare the simple prayer of King David with the simple prayer of King Solomon. Then ask yourself one simple question. "Do I have any unfinished prayers prayed in my life?" If you do have a number of unfinished prayers then ask the Lord to teach you how to finish your prayers. I believe that a finished prayer is learning how to pray moment-by-moment.

Read prayerfully, Solomon's prayer. As you read his prayer ask the Holy Spirit of God to sharpen your ability to listen in a new and different way. Listen with your heart and not with your head. Listen quietly:

> *When Solomon had finished praying, fire came down from heaven and consumed the burnt offering and the sacrifices; and the glory of the Lord filled the temple. And the priests could not enter the house of the Lord, because the glory of the Lord had filled the Lord's house. When all the children of Israel saw how the fire came down, and the glory of the Lord on the temple, they bowed their faces to the ground on the pavement, and worshiped and praised the Lord, saying: "For He is good, For His mercy endures forever." Then the king and all the people offered sacrifices before the LORD. King Solomon offered a sacrifice of twenty-two thousand bulls and one hundred and twenty thousand sheep. So the king and all the people dedicated the house of God*
>
> 2 CHRONICLES 7:1-5

Solomon consecrated the temple of the LORD. Solomon and the people of God celebrated joyfully with glad hearts and sincere hearts for all the good things that the LORD had done for David and Solomon and for His people, Israel. The Scripture declared at the close of 2 Chronicles 7:1-5, these finishing words following Solomon prayer. "So the king and all the people dedicated the house of God." Notice that Solomon did not dedicate the Lord's house apart from praying. Prayer must always precede divine approval. King Solomon's simple prayer led him on a path of divine approval.

Prayer Approval

Solomon's prayer was good, but God still had to give His approval for what Solomon had done in building the temple of the Lord. Solomon's secret in obtaining the Lord's approval was connected to finishing his prayer and finishing his task. Solomon finished both responsibilities. How do you know a man of prayer? A man of prayer is a man who is faithful to completing his task. Solomon's faithfulness to prayer and his hard work was the two ingredients to his success. We are to pray and work. This was the proper order, pray and work. Solomon did not work and pray, he prayed and worked. Prayer must always precede work. In other words, prayer is equivalent to operating in the Spirit's power. Work is equivalent to operating in the realm of human effort.

If we want to be successful in our ministry of the Word of God–preaching for Spiritual Awakening–then we must prayer hard and work hard. Hard prayer and hard work was Solomon's right and left punch for success.

It is one thing to obey man; it is another thing to obey the Lord. I want to challenge you to listen to what God's Word says. It is time for you to read what the Scriptures says in the context of learning to pray hard and work hard to achieve success in the work of the Lord. Read every last word. Pray and read.

> *Thus Solomon finished the house of the LORD and the king's house; and Solomon successfully accomplished all that came into his heart to make in the house of the LORD and in his own house. Then the LORD appeared to Solomon by night, and said to him: "I have heard your prayer, and have chosen this place for Myself as a house of sacrifice. When I shut up heaven and there is no rain, or command the locusts to devour the land, or send pestilence among My people, if My people who are called by My name will humble themselves, and pray and seek My face, and turn from their wicked ways, then I will hear from heaven, and will forgive their sin and heal their land. Now My eyes will be open and My ears attentive to prayer made in this place.*
>
> 2 CHRONICLES 7:11-15

The Lord concludes His response to Solomon's simple prayer with these words. "Now My eyes will be open and My ears attentive to prayer made in this place." What was so profound about this place? I believe it was the place where the Lord had given His sacred approval. Any place where the Lord has given His sacred approval is the right place. That is why the Apostle Paul said, in 1 Corinthians 2:2 (NIV), "For I [Paul] resolved to know nothing while I was with you except Jesus Christ and Him crucified." Paul knew that sacred place. It was the place of Christ's approval. It was a place of answered prayer.

The Lord knows how to answer our prayers. The Lord wants us to pray. If we would simply pray, the Lord would simply respond and resolve our deepest concerns in due season. Timing is everything to God. We must learn how to wait for the right time. Getting ahead of God's timing can be hazardous to the health of our souls. Once we have discerned the proper timing, we are to move expeditiously to a point of consummation. Waiting one second too late could forfeit God's best in our lives. Now it is time for you to prayerfully read the words of the proverbial writer. Possibly the writer was King Solomon. Despite the human author, the divine author was the Lord God Almighty. Scripture simply states these words to you and me concerning timing:

There is a time for everything, and a season for every activity under heaven: a time to be born and a time to die, a time to plant and a time to uproot, a time to kill and a time to heal, a time to tear down and a time to build, a time to weep and a time to laugh, a time to mourn and a time to dance, a time to scatter stones and a time to gather them, a time to embrace and a time to refrain, a time to search and a time to give up, a time to keep and a time to throw away, a time to tear and a time to mend, a time to be silent and a time to speak, a time to love and a time to hate, a time for war and a time for peace.

ECCLESIASTES **3:1-8**, NIV

There is a time for everything, even prayer! The Lord answered Israel's prayer and resolved their issues! When does God do His best work in prayer?

First, when prayer comes from a humble heart. God's people were in a place and time in their lives when they needed to clearly understand that God meant what He said. God was serious. He was not playing power games with His people. What made matters worse was that His people failed to realize the eternal consequences of their ungodly actions. Yet, God, being a God of love, did not turn His ear from the prayer of His people. God wants to hear our prayers. He desires to hear the hearts of His people. That's good news.

When we hear the good news of the gospel of Jesus Christ, we ought to respond joyfully. We ought to be abundantly grateful to Almighty God for what He has done and is doing on our account. So, my question to you is this. What are you going to do to humble your heart, so that God does not have to crush your heart into humble submission? What are you going to do now? Not tomorrow. Not next week, but right now.

We ought to celebrate when we hear the voice of the Lord say these words to us. In **2** Chronicles **7:14**, the Scripture says, "…if My people, who are called by My name, will humble themselves…" A humble heart is God's palace: "I dwell in the high and holy place, with him who has a contrite and humble spirit" (Isaiah **57:15**b). In Numbers **12:3**, the Bible says, "Now the man Moses was very humble." In Proverbs **3:34**, the Bible says, "He…gives grace to the humble." In Ephesians **4:2** (NIV), the Bible says, "Be completely humble and gentle…" In James **4:10** (NIV), the Bible says, "Humble yourselves before the Lord, and He will lift you up." In **1** Peter **5:7** (NIV), the Bible says, "Humble yourselves, therefore, under God's mighty hand, that He may lift you up in due time." This ought to cause us to shout hallelujah, praise the Lord, thank you, Jesus. My question for us today is this: What did Jesus do for you that would cause you to shout and bless His name? I know what He did for me and I'm going to praise Him for giving me a humble heart and not a haughty heart. What about you? What are you going to do? When does God do His best work in prayer? It is when prayer comes from a humble heart.

Second, when does prayer do its best work? I honestly believe it is when prayer comes from a heavy heart. Solomon prayed with a heavy heart. He prayed so hard until it caught the attention of God. Yet, God's people still had not gotten the complete picture. It's a shame when we fail to take the time to listen to God. Who in their right mind would ignore God? Israel did. They turned their back on God. But God did not give up on His people. He felt their heavy heart. In 2 Chronicles 7:14, it says, "…and prayer…" Jesus said, in Matthew 11:28-30 (NIV), "Come to Me, all you who are weary and burdened, and I will give you rest. Take My yoke upon you and learn from Me, for I am gentle and humble in heart, and you will find rest for your souls. For My yoke is easy and My burden is light." Have you considered the nature of your heart? Do you believe you possess a heart of humility? Do you have a humble heart? Prayer is what it is all about. Prayer does its best work when we work prayer. Prayer works. Oh, yes it does. I know that it does. I have tried it for myself and it works.

I remember the story of the little boy who was afraid of the dark. He pleaded with his mom and dad, "Please don't turn off the light, Mommy and Daddy, I am so afraid." This went on for a number of months, until one day, the little boy's father told him, "Son, since you are so afraid, I will lie down with you to keep you company to chase your fears away." As time would have it and the little boy grew to maturity, he said, to his father, "Father, I'm okay now. I am no longer afraid of the dark." "What caused this change?" his father asked. The little boy responded, "I was taught today in Vacation Bible school that every Christian has a light inside of them and that light is Jesus. I asked my teacher, 'Tell me how I might get this light?' My teacher helped me understand that the reason why I was afraid of the dark was that I needed Jesus in my heart. She said, 'Once you receive Jesus in your heart, His light will overshadow the darkness everywhere.' 'Everywhere, I asked.' She said, 'Everywhere.' I said, 'Even in my room?' She said, 'Yes, even in your room.'"

"Father, I got a living, eternal light shining in my heart today. I will never fear the dark again. Father, according to the Bible, Jesus said, 'I am the light of the world.' And I am to let my light shine so that others can see Jesus in my life. Father, I have my new light on. Can't you see how bright it is?"

When prayer does its best work, our heavy hearts of fear will be flooded with the light of the Lord Jesus Christ. Prayer does its best work when it comes from a humble heart, a heavy heart, and a hungry heart. God fed Israel manna in the wilderness. That was good food. But what Israel needed now is living bread–bread not only for the body, but for the soul. However, they often refused to eat once it was provided. God will provide the bread for any hungry soul, but He will not make us eat it. We must decide to eat it for ourselves.

Unfortunately, even if we had the human power to take care of ourselves, it still would not be good enough. We need something beyond us; we need the grace of God, the work of His Holy Spirit to help us do what we cannot do in our own strength. We need divine intervention to feed our hungry hearts. In 2 Chronicles 7:14, God said, "…and seek My face…"

You will never be successful until you seek the face of God. What does this mean? You must enter into God's presence. You must spend time with God. You must be hungry for the true manna. You must hunger for the Living Bread. That bread is none other than Jesus.

When Adolph Hitler occupied Germany with the iron fist of evil, people were denied the ability to eat like human beings. People literally ate whatever they could find. Many people starved to death before the Allies liberated those people herded like dumb animals into numerous concentration camps. For those of us who have received Jesus Christ as our Savior and Lord, Hitler may starve our bodies, but never our souls. Our souls are eternally nourished by the Living Water and the Living Bread. Jesus is that bread from heaven. "Bread of heaven, bread of heaven, feed me until I want no more."

Third, God does His best work in prayer, when prayer comes from a hungry heart. 2 Chronicles 7:14, says, "…and seek My face…" In Romans 7:18, the Apostle Paul took a quiet inner look at himself. In summary, Paul appears to be a perplexed man. He comes across as if he is losing his mind. Yet the opposite is indeed the case. Paul was in touch with who and what he was before the eyes of the Lord Jesus Christ. Paul knew what he knew. Far too many times we are preoccupied with the wrong preoccupation. We are often preoccupied with ourselves and not our Lord. Paul changed his occupation to being preoccupied with God. We must never become so preoccupied with self until we forget our Savior and our Lord, Jesus Christ. Read now the words of Paul as he views himself before a holy, righteous, and perfect God. Paul says,

I know that nothing good lives in me, that is, in my sinful nature. For I have the desire to do what is good, but I cannot carry it out. For what

I do is not the good I want to do; no, the evil I do not want to do–this I keep on doing. Now if I do what I do not want to do, it is no longer I who do it, but it is sin living in me that does it.
ROMANS **7:18-20**, NIV

Paul identified his problem to the tee. He said "For what I do is not the good I want to do; no, the evil I do no want to do–this I keep on doing." Paul realized his problem on one hand and then his need on the other. Read carefully and prayerfully Paul words to the church. Paul uncovers his deep pain for the salvation of others. As you read Paul's words, simply place yourself in Paul's position. Then re-read Paul's words and place yourself in the position of the hearers:

Brothers, my heart's desire and prayer to God for the Israelites is that they may be saved. For I can testify about them that they are zealous for God, but their zeal is not based on knowledge. Since they did not know the righteousness that comes from God and sought to establish their own, they did not submit to God's righteousness.
ROMANS **10:1-4**, NIV

Preaching for spiritual awakening is not simply about performance preaching. It is about the power of prayer in preaching. It is about learning how to submit to the Lord Jesus Christ. Zealous preaching in one thing, but submissive preaching is another. Paul said, "Since they did not know the righteousness that comes from God and sought to establish their own, they did not submit to God's righteousness." When we submit to the righteousness of Christ in prayer–Supernatural Power will be the result in our preaching of the gospel of Jesus Christ. Let us remember that Christ is the end of the law so that there may be righteousness for everyone who believes. When does God do His best work in prayer? It is when prayer comes from a hungry heart.

Fourth and finally, God does His best work in prayer when prayer comes from a holy heart. In **2** Chronicles **7:14**, the Bible says, "…and turn from their wicked ways, then will I hear from heaven and will forgive their sin and will heal their land." In Exodus **20:8**, the Bible says, "Remember the Sabbath day, to keep it holy." In Leviticus **19:2**, the Bible says, "You shall be holy, for I the LORD your God am holy." In **1** Peter **1:16**, the Bible says, "Be holy, for I am holy." As you read Isaiah **6:3-5**, notice the phrase "…the whole earth is full of His glory!" God made man from the dust of the earth and breathed into him His Spirit and man become a living soul. Isaiah learned a simple lesson. God was holy and he was not. Read Isaiah's experience in the presence of the Lord God Almighty. The Bible says,

> *Holy, holy, holy is the LORD of hosts; the whole earth is full of His glory!" And the posts of the door were shaken by the voice of him who cried out, and the house was filled with smoke. So I said: "Woe is me, for I am undone! Because I am a man of unclean lips, and I dwell in the midst of a people of unclean lips; for my eyes have seen the King, The LORD of hosts."*
>
> Isaiah **6:3-5**

A Final Word

When our hearts are humble, heavy, hungry, and holy, we will pray with power! Church, we need to pray! We need not words, but divine communication. Divine communication is conversing from the heart of man to the heart of heaven–a connection unburdened and untainted by sin and human pride. Pray with power.

Is this church a powerful, praying church? Not just a church that says prayers, but a powerful praying church? There are many churches that say prayers, but not every church is a powerful, praying church! So, why are there so many churches that do not possess a powerful prayer life? The reason is unconfessed, unrepentant sin!

> *If we claim to be without sin, we deceive ourselves and the truth is not in us. If we confess our sins, He is faithful and just and will forgive us our sins and purify us from all unrighteousness. If we claim we have not sinned, we make Him out to be a liar and His word has no place in our lives.*
>
> 1 John **1:8-10**, NIV

That is why in Matthew **4:17**b (NIV), Jesus said, "Repent, for the kingdom of heaven is near." Let us be reminded that "Repent" is the first word of the gospel.[8]

If you need revival in your life, in your marriage, in your family, in your finances, or in your faith, in your home, and even in your church–come to Jesus! Church, do you believe America needs revival? But, when will God send revival? The Bible says, "Judgment begins at the House of God." When the

---

8 Richard Owen Roberts, *Repentance: The First Word of the Gospel* (Crossway Book, 2002), 23.

church gets right with God, revival will come. We need a fresh encounter with God before His patience runs out. Henry Blackaby and Claude King write, "Some people have developed a theology that releases them from any personal accountability for sin once they are saved. They argue that God does not punish those who are redeemed and forgiven by the blood of Jesus."[9] They're wrong.

Leaders, we are the ones that God is going to come and reprimand, discipline, and chasten. Saints, we need an authentic revival stimulus package for the American soul. Ask yourself the following questions then read the closing words of the writer of the Chronicles in chapter 7:15-16. First are your ears open to hearing what the Lord is saying to you? Are your eyes attentive to seeing the work of the Lord around you today? Is your heart tender and humble before the Lord? Are you ready to experience a genuine revival in your soul? Read the Chronicler in his own words.

Now My eyes will be open and My ears attentive to the prayers offered in this place. I have chosen and consecrated this temple so that My Name may be there forever. My eyes and My heart will always be there.
2 CHRONICLES 7:15-16, NIV

Jesus said in Matthew 21:13, "It is written, 'My house shall be called a house of prayer.'" A house of prayer is a house with humble-hearted people. A house of prayer is a house with heavy-hearted people. A house of prayer is a house with hungry-hearted people. And finally, a house of prayer is a house with holy-hearted people.

But, who is this fifth ingredient of a powerful praying church? Who is our revival stimulus person? His name is Jesus and He humbled His heart and He become sin for sinful man! Jesus had a heavy heart that led Him to weep! Jesus had a hungry heart and He became living bread! Jesus had a holy heart and He died for you and me! Andrew Murray summarizes His death in a small book titled *The Power of the Blood of Jesus*. Murray preaches in his closing chapter that there are heavenly rewards through the precious blood of the Lord Jesus Christ. "There is between the sprinkling of the blood and the joys of heaven and that a true intimate connection with the blood on earth will enable the believer while still on earth to share the joy and glory of heaven."[10]

9 Henry T. Blackaby and Claude V. King, *Fresh Encounter: Experiencing God Through Prayer, Humility and a Heartfelt Desire to Know Him* (Nashville, TN: Broadman and Holman Publishers, 1996), 97.
10 Andrew Murray, *The Power of the Blood of Jesus* (New Kensington, PA: Whitaker

How is your heart? Do you have a humble heart? Do you have a heavy heart? Do you have a hungry heart? Do you have a holy heart? Jesus had a humble heart. It was so humbled that He took on sin for us! Jesus had a heavy heart. It was so heavy that He wept! Jesus had a hungry heart. It was so hungry that He became living bread! Jesus had a holy heart. It was so holy that He died for you and me!

House, 1993), 167.

Chapter 9

The Giant Killer

Don't Send a Boy to Do a Man's Job

David said to the Philistine, "You come against me with sword and spear and javelin, but I come against you in the name of the Lord Almighty, the God of the armies of Israel, whom you have defied."

1 SAMUEL **17:45**, NIV

When Will God Send Revival?

Could it be that God will send revival when the magnitude of our God within us is greater than the magnitude of our giants against us? I pray that God will send a life-changing, soul-stirring, spirit-anointed revival! The challenges you will experience in reading this chapter on "The Giant Killer" will be in three areas. First, you will assume your knowledge of the Scripture and you will rush through the passages as if you already know them well enough to blaze through each Scriptural passage employing past understandings. Don't do this. Read every last word. Don't assume that you already know what the passage is saying to you. If you do not read every last word you will surly miss your blessing.

Your second challenge will be similar to your first challenge. You will be tempted to pray and ask the Lord to unlock the Scriptures you are reading. Chapter 9 is not for the academic minded person. You must be hungry and thirsty for the righteousness of God. You will have to seek God's insights even as you read or read what you have read for many years. Don't allow prior insights to rob you of potential deeper insights and illuminations embedded in each and every passage. Take the time to read with passion and patience.

"A priori" and "a posteriori" knowledge is good. A *priori* knowledge is existing knowledge in the mind prior to and independent of experience. Knowledge of this sort requires no investigation (Dictionary.com). One assumes they know. Thus the need to learn is extinguished. A person with this type of knowledge assumption will not read each and every passage of Scripture because he or she has no need to do so. He or she assumes prior understanding, thus to re-read what is already known is a waste of time, energy, and intellectual effort. This is dangerous. I pray that you do not approach chapter 9 with a *priori* knowledge.

At the other end of the spectrum of knowledge and understanding is "a posteriori" knowledge. *A posteriori* type of knowledge is based upon a form of knowledge or understanding that is based upon actual observation or upon experimental data: an *a posteriori* argument that derives the theory from the evidence (Dictionary.com). A person with this type of knowledge base would say, "You've got to prove to me from your evidence what you mean or what you are saying." What I have chosen to do in chapter 9 is to allow the Scriptures to speak for me. I will expound when necessary but my expositions will be decisive, precise, and succinct. I want you to experience chapter 9 from the heart of the Scriptures. I am convinced that this narrative will speak for itself.

Now let us engage with the Lord and see with a new perspective what happened to David, a boy faced with a man sized job. In 1 Samuel the Bible records this amazing story,

• Encamped in the Valley of Elah

And Saul and the men of Israel were gathered together, and they encamped in the Valley of Elah, and drew up in battle array against the Philistines. The Philistines stood on a mountain on one side, and Israel stood on a mountain on the other side, with a valley between them.

• Goliath from Gath

And a champion went out from the camp of the Philistines, named Goliath, from Gath, whose height was six cubits and a span. He had a bronze helmet on his head, and he was armed with a coat of mail, and the weight of the coat was five thousand shekels of bronze. And he had bronze armor on his legs and a bronze javelin between his shoulders. Now the staff of his spear was like a weaver's beam, and his iron spearhead weighed six hundred shekels; and a shield-bearer went before him. Then he stood and cried out to the armies of Israel, and said to them, "Why have you come out to line up for battle? Am I not a Philistine, and you the servants of Saul? Choose a man for yourselves, and let him come down to me. If he is able to fight with me and kill me, then we will be your servants. But if I prevail against him and kill him, then you shall be our servants and serve us." And the Philistine said, "I defy the armies of Israel this day; give me a man, that we may fight together." When Saul and all Israel heard these words of the Philistine, they were dismayed and greatly afraid.

1 SAMUEL 17:2-11

• David son of Jesse

Now David was the son of that Ephrathite of Bethlehem Judah, whose name was Jesse, and who had eight sons. And the man was old, advanced in years, in the days of Saul. The three oldest sons of Jesse had gone to follow Saul to the battle. The names of his three sons who went to the battle were Eliab the firstborn, next to him Abinadab, and the third Shammah. David was the youngest. And the three oldest followed Saul. But David occasionally went and returned from Saul to feed his father's sheep at Bethlehem. And the Philistine drew near and presented himself forty days, morning and evening."

1 SAMUEL 17:12-16

• Saul's Rewards

So the men of Israel said, "Have you seen this man who has come up? Surely he has come up to defy Israel; and it shall be that the man who kills him the king will enrich with great riches, will give him his daughter, and give his father's house exemption from taxes in Israel."

1 SAMUEL 17:25

• David the Little Shepherd Boy

Then David said to Saul, "Let no man's heart fail because of him; your servant will go and fight with this Philistine." And Saul said to David, "You are not able to go against this Philistine to fight with him; for you are a youth, and he a man of war from his youth." But David said to Saul, "Your servant used to keep his father's sheep, and when a lion or a bear came and took a lamb out of the flock, I went out after it and struck it, and delivered the lamb from its mouth; and when it arose against me, I caught it by its beard, and struck and killed it. Your servant has killed both lion and bear; and this uncircumcised Philistine will be like one of them, seeing he has defied the armies of the Living God." Moreover David said, "The Lord, who delivered me from the paw of the lion and from the paw of the bear, He will deliver me from the hand of this Philistine." And Saul said to David, "Go, and the Lord be with you!"

1 SAMUEL 17:32-37

• Goliath's View of the Shepherd Boy

And when the Philistine looked about and saw David, he disdained him; for he was only a youth, ruddy and good-looking. So the Philistine said to David, "Am I a dog, that you come to me with sticks?" And the Philistine cursed David by his gods. And the Philistine said to David, "Come to me, and I will give your flesh to the birds of the air and the beasts of the field!"

• David's View of His God

Then David said to the Philistine, "You come to me with a sword, with a spear, and with a javelin. But I come to you in the name of the Lord of hosts, the God of the armies of Israel, whom you have defied."

1 SAMUEL 17:42-45

• Saul's View of the Shepherd Boy

And Saul said to him, "Whose son are you, young man?"

• David the son of Jesse the Bethlehemite–the Giant Killer

So David answered, "I am the son of your servant Jesse the Bethlehemite."

1 SAMUEL 17:58

The Sword and Spear vs. His Name and Nature

The key verse in the text is 1 Samuel 17:45, "Then David said to the Philistine, 'You come to me with a sword, with a spear, and with a javelin. But I come to you in the name of the Lord of hosts, the God of the armies of Israel, whom you have defied.'"

Big Problems, Small God; Big God, Small Problems

The Bigger They Are, the Harder They Fall!

What's wrong with this picture? Here we have in the text today, a boy suiting up to do a job that demanded, dictated, and denoted the necessity of a grown man doing grown-up stuff. However, there was no grown man in the camp of Israel who had enough courage to stand up to a defiant, disrespectful, deplorable, dogmatic, distasteful, deranged and demanding giant, named Goliath of Gath.

Why would God decide to use a little shepherd boy, by the name of David, son of Jesse, to do a job that was the size of a grown, mature, and experienced warrior? It is not understandable. Humanly, it is a shame that God had to send a boy to do a man's job. However, the truth of the matter is, it is not the size of a man that denotes the magnitude of his God. Rather, it is the size of the Spirit of God that dwells in the heart of the man of God that magnifies the size of the man's God. You see, David was a boy with a God-sized spirit. In other words, it was the magnitude of David's God that made him victorious. In short, David possessed a child-like spirit in a God-sized body.

He did not need King Saul's man-sized armor; David was suited up with the God-sized armor of the Lord of lords and the Kings of kings.

God will never send a boy to do a man-sized job–God does send a God-sized boy who possesses a child-like spirit to do a man-sized job. For it was in this child-sized boy that God defeated a giant-sized giant with a child-like spirit in a God-sized body. In the economy of God, man's big is always small, whereas God's small is always bigger!

What we need, today, in the church of the Lord Jesus Christ is men, women, boys, and girls who possess a child-like spirit to deal with giant-sized problems not only in our world, in our nation, in our churches, in our homes, in our marriages, in our schools, in our government, but most of all in our prideful, arrogant, and non-serving spirits. What we really need in the church of the Lord Jesus Christ is a God-sent revival from a God-sized God to straighten up the saints and a God-sized God to send a spiritual awakening to save lost and hell-bound souls.

In other words, when our spirits are too big, our God is too small, but when our spirits are child-like then our God is God-like and then nothing will be impossible for our God. "For we can do all things through Christ who strengthens us." We serve an awesome God! We serve a God who can do anything but fail! He is the God of all gods, His is the Lord of all lords, and He is everything that we need today to defeat all of the giants in our life for His glory, His honor, and His praise.

J.B. Phillips, in his little book, *Your God Is Too Small*, said: "Small God, Big Problems; Big God small problems."[1] In other words, "The bigger they are the harder they fall!" So, "How big is your problem?" Israel obviously thought that they had a big problem in going to war with the Philistines.

Every day the giant Goliath went out and defied the name of the Lord. Cursing God to His face and daring God to be God–literally, pointing his finger in the face of God and saying to God, "I dare You to be who You said You are!"

In All Your Getting, Get Understanding

If Israel believed that they served the One True God, then why was there no one in the camp of King Saul's army confident enough to stand up to challenge the giant Goliath? It was because the they feared Goliath more than God! They had a small-god mentality, which caused them to have a giant-sized problem. In 1 Samuel 17:11 the Bible states, "When Saul and all Israel heard these words of the Philistine, they were dismayed and greatly afraid.." Small god, big problem; Big God, small problem!

The Story

But, wait a minute. The story isn't over. Did you not know that the Lord always has somebody bigger than the problem at hand? Most often our solution comes in small packages, wrapped in a child-like spirit to give our giant-sized problem a divine haircut at the head level. In other words, God needed a man with a child-like spirit to complete a giant-sized problem. Big God; small problems; small god, Big Problems!

In 1 Samuel 17:32, [David was that man with a child-like spirit] the Bible states, "David said to Saul, 'Let no man's heart fail because of him; your servant will go and fight with this Philistine.'" Now, get this…

There are seven irrefutable, profoundly simple, child-like rules we need to know when we are facing and fighting giant-sized problems in our life:

• **Rule 1: Don't lose heart: Go face and fight your giant right now.**

> (v. 32) "David said to Saul…our servant will go and fight with this Philistine."

---

1 J. B. Phillips, *Your God is Too Small* (New York, NY: Touchstone, 2004, 11.

• **Rule 2: Don't believe what others say about your ability to face and fight your giant.**

(v. **33**) Saul said, "David, 'You are not able to go against this Philistine to fight with him; for you are a youth, and he a man of war from his youth.'"

• **Rule 3: Remember your past victories in facing and fighting your giant.**

(vv. **34-37**a) David said, to Saul, "But David said to Saul, "Your servant used to keep his father's sheep, and when a lion or a bear came and took a lamb out of the flock, I went out after it and struck it, and delivered the lamb from its mouth; and when it arose against me, I caught it by its beard, and struck and killed it. Your servant has killed both lion and bear; and this uncircumcised Philistine will be like one of them, seeing he has defied the armies of the living God. Moreover David said, "The LORD, who delivered me from the paw of the lion and from the paw of the bear, He will deliver me from the hand of this Philistine."

• **Rule 4: Don't wear another man's armor when facing and fighting your giant.**

(vv. **38-40**) "So Saul clothed David with his armor, and he put a bronze helmet on his head; he also clothed him with a coat of mail. David fastened his sword to his armor and tried to walk, for he had not tested them. And David said to Saul, "I cannot walk with these, for I have not tested them." So David took them off. Then he took his staff in his hand; and he chose for himself five smooth stones from the brook, and put them in a shepherd's bag, in a pouch which he had, and his sling was in his hand. And he drew near to the Philistine.

With all your weight, learn how to lean into your giants.

• **Rule 5: Don't ever forget that the Lord is with you when facing and fighting your giant.**

(vv. **45-47**) "Then David said to the Philistine, 'You come to me with a sword, with a spear, and with a javelin. But I come to you in the name of the LORD of hosts, the God of the armies of Israel, whom you have defied. This day the LORD will deliver you into my hand, and I will strike you and take your head from you. And this day I will give the carcasses of the camp of the Philistines to the birds of the air and the wild beasts of the earth, that all the earth may know that there is a God in Israel. Then all this assembly shall know that the LORD does not save with sword and spear; for the battle is the LORD'S, and

He will give you into our hands.'"

• Rule 6: When facing and fighting your giant, learn how to lunge or run into the path and power of your giant.

(vv. **48-49**) "So it was, when the Philistine arose and came and drew near to meet David, that David hurried and ran toward the army to meet the Philistine. Then David put his hand in his bag and took out a stone; and he slung it and struck the Philistine in his forehead, so that the stone sank into his forehead, and he fell on his face to the earth. "

• Rule 7: Last but not least, make sure when facing and fighting your giant that you cut off his head and kill him.

(vv. **50-51**) "So David prevailed over the Philistine with a sling and a stone, and struck the Philistine and killed him. But there was no sword in the hand of David. Therefore David ran and stood over the Philistine, took his sword and drew it out of its sheath and killed him, and cut off his head with it. And when the Philistines saw that their champion was dead, they fled."

Did you get these seven irrefutable rules for dealing with your giants? David did, with a child-like spirit. He decapitated his giant-sized problem with the help of his giant-sized God with a sling and a stone, not a gun or a bow!

Do Not Negotiate with a Giant

David defeated the giant Goliath with a sling and a stone. Did you hear what the Bible said? David defeated the giant Goliath with a sling and a stone? A stone! One smooth stone!

•Jesus Christ the Stone in Zion

As it is written: "See, I lay in Zion a stone that causes men to stumble and a rock that makes them fall, and the one who trusts in Him will never be put to shame."
ROMANS **9:33**, NIV

• Jesus Christ the Capstone

Now to you who believe, this stone is precious. But to those who do not believe, "The stone the builders rejected has become the capstone. A stone that causes men to stumble and a rock that makes them fall."
1 PETER **2:7-8**, NIV

They stumble because they disobey the message—which is also what they were destined for.

• We are a Chosen People

But you are a chosen people, a royal priesthood, a holy nation, a people belonging to God, that you may declare the praises of Him who called you out of darkness into His wonderful light. Once you were not a people, but now you are the people of God; once you had not received mercy, but now you have received mercy.

1 Peter **2:9-10**, NIV

That's Victory!

I heard an old, old story, how a Savior came from glory, how He gave His life on Calvary to save a wretch like me; I heard about His groaning, of His precious blood's atoning, then I repented of my sins and won the victory.

Chorus: O victory in Jesus, My Savior, forever. He sought me and bought me with His redeeming blood; He loved me 'ere I knew Him And all my love is due Him,He plunged me to victory, beneath the cleansing flood.

I heard about His healing, of His cleansing pow'r revealing. How He made the lame to walk again and caused the blind to see; and then I cried, "Dear Jesus, come and heal my broken spirit," And somehow Jesus came and brought to me the victory.

I heard about a mansion He has built for me in glory. And I heard about the streets of gold beyond the crystal sea; about the angels singing, and the old redemption story, and some sweet day I'll sing up there the song of victory.[2]

We've Got the Victory

We have the victory! David defeated his giant and decapitated him with his own sword. Ephesians **6:17** says, "And take the helmet of salvation, and the sword of the Spirit, which is the word of God." Hebrews says:

---

2 *Victory in Jesus*, Words and Music by E.M. Bartlett, © 1939 – Administrated by Integrated Copyright Group, Inc., All rights reserved.

- ### The Word of God: A Double-Edged Sword

For the word of God is living and powerful, and sharper than any two-edged sword, piercing even to the division of soul and spirit, and of joints and marrow, and is a discerner of the thoughts and intents of the heart. And there is no creature hidden from His sight, but all things are naked and open to the eyes of Him to whom we must give account.
HEBREWS **4:12-13**

- ### David Discovered His Help from on High: The Hills

Psalm **121** says:

I will lift up my eyes to the hills–from whence comes my help? My help comes from the Lord, Who made heaven and earth. He will not allow your foot to be moved; He who keeps you will not slumber. Behold, He who keeps Israel shall neither slumber nor sleep. The Lord is your keeper; the Lord is your shade at your right hand. The sun shall not strike you by day, nor the moon by night. The Lord shall preserve you from all evil; He shall preserve your soul. The Lord shall preserve your going out and your coming in from this time forth, and even forevermore.
PSALM **121:1-8**

- ### David the Giant Killer: A Boy Doing a Man's Job

In **1** Samuel **17:54**, the Bible says, "David took the Philistine's head and brought it to Jerusalem, and he put the Philistine's weapons in his own tent."

- ### David's Rewards

And Saul said to him, "Whose son are you, young man?" So David answered, "I am the son of your servant Jesse the Bethlehemite."
1 SAMUEL **17:58**

The Savior and the Serpent

In the same way, Jesus, who was wrapped in swaddling clothes lying in a manager cut off the head of the Serpent at Calvary! *The same Serpent* that deceived Eve and Adam, *the same Serpent* that caused Cain to kill his brother Abel, *the same Serpent* that caused the flood, *the same Serpent* that caused Sodom and Gomorrah to be destroyed, *the same Serpent* that caused Jacob to steal Esau's birthright, *the same Serpent* that caused Israel to wander in the wilderness for forty years, *the same Serpent* that allowed Job to lose everything, was *the same Serpent* that Jesus met after fasting forty days and forty nights.

It was the Serpent of old. However, Jesus crushed and decapitated the Serpent, Lucifer, and He has his head in His Hand. "It is finished!" The Resurrection cut off his head. The tomb is empty, Jesus is alive!

The Public Enemy of Pride

So, the giant of pride has been beheaded. The giant of impatience has been beheaded. The giant of anger has been beheaded. The giant of fear has been beheaded. The giant of sin has been beheaded. The giant of disobedience has been beheaded. The giant of materialism has been beheaded. The giant of self-righteousness has been beheaded. The giant of unforgiveness has been beheaded. The giants of death, hell, and the grave have all been beheaded. Is there a giant in your life that needs a close haircut?

Small god, Big Problems! Big God, small problems! Do you possess a child-like spirit?

Chapter 10

We Need To Live Up To Our Name

Rejoice in the Lord always. I will say it again: Rejoice!

PHILIPPIANS **4:4**, NIV

When will God send revival? I believe that God will send revival when unconditional joy floods the church of the Lord Jesus Christ each and every Lord's Day. I believe that God will send a revival that will sweep clean the hearts of sinful men, purge out the ungodly minds of fallen men, and then saturate the parched flesh of the souls of men in order to send revival. In Philippians **4:4** (NIV), the Apostle Paul said it best: "Rejoice in the Lord always. I will say it again: Rejoice!" If we are to preach for spiritual awakening, we must do it with unconditional joy, so rejoice anyway! It's a great day in the Lord! We need to live up to our name.

Your Character Should Be Joy!

We have unconditional joy that allows us to rejoice anyway. The only way you can say, "It's a great day in the Lord," is because of true joy! What would happen if every church, pastor, staff member, deacon and spiritual leader, every missionary, and every association of churches focused more on God than on being emotionally happy? *Happiness* is an emotion that changes according to life circumstances. *Joy* is an everlasting choice to see things through the sovereign eyes of the Lord Jesus Christ. Let us rejoice in the Lord on a daily bases. In other words, in the words of a great preacher, "It's a great day in the Lord," because we have joy!

Godly Fragrance

There were two ladies in Philippi; Euodia and Syntyche. The problem was that they were fighting. Euodia's name means "fragrance or a prosperous journey" and Syntyche's name means "a pleasant acquaintance." Here we have *prosperous fragrance* and *pleasant acquaintance* fighting in the church. *Prosperous Fragrance* was unwilling to get along with *Pleasant Acquaintance* and *Pleasant Acquaintance* refused to get along with *Prosperous Fragrance*. *Prosperous Fragrance* and *Pleasant Acquaintance* were not living up to their names. It is really a shame, when we as Christians do not live up to our names as well. It is a shame when we as preachers, pastors, Bible teachers, ministers of music, men's and women's leaders, youth leaders, children's leaders, denominational leaders, black people, red people, and white people, who declare the name of Jesus, can't have church together in the name of Jesus and can't reconcile.

The Apostle Paul learned about *Prosperous Fragrance* and *Pleasant Acquaintance* quarreling in the House of God. Paul pleaded for their reconciliation. He wanted *Pleasant Acquaintance* and *Prosperous Fragrance* to experience unconditional joy and simply rejoice anyway! He wanted them to live up to their name.

The time is now that we need cooperation between *Godly Fragrance* and *Spiritual Pleasance*. Saints, we need to keep filling our churches with *Godly Fragrance* and *Spiritual Pleasance* so that we might bring people to Jesus to be saved and so that our churches may grow in Spirit and in Truth. Then we would be able to say, "It's a great day in the Lord."

Therefore, "rejoice in the Lord always!" Two times in his Philippian Letter Paul urges the Christians at Philippi to "rejoice in the Lord" (**3:1** and **4:4**). The second time he repeats the call twice, "Rejoice…again I say rejoice!" And he added the word *always*. The joy of the Christian life is not of a passing quality. Rejoicing in the Lord is not to be reserved for special times of worship or praise. It is to be uninterrupted and unbroken fellowship of joy, peace, love, thanksgiving, and celebration to the God of Heaven and Earth, through His redemptive Son, the Lord Jesus Christ. Jesus![1]

What is the solution to restore, resurrect, and revive the relationship between *Prosperous Fragrance* and *Pleasant Acquaintance*? The solution comes when we "Rejoice in the Lord, always" because we remember, as a child of God, that it is always "a great day in the Lord."

So, "How do we do it?" How do we get *Prosperous Fragrance* and *Pleasant Acquaintance* to stop quarrelling with each other so that we can get about

---

1 Lloyd J. Ogilvie and Maxie D. Dunnam, *The Communicator's Commentary: Galatians, Ephesians, Phillippians, Colossians, Philemon* (Waco, Texas: Word Books Publisher, 1982), 310.

our Father's business and make disciples of Jesus Christ to produce healthy, whole, Spirit-filled, Spirit-anointed, God-fearing, joyful, loving, compassionate, evangelistic, missional, serving, sacrificing, surrendering, supportive, cooperative, grace-filled and mercy-driven healthy churches to go into an unhealthy world with the healing gospel of Jesus Christ for the glory of God Almighty? How do we do it? How do we maintain "a great day in the Lord?"

First, we must identify the right location to point our unconditional joy!

Paul says, in Philippians **4**, that we must point our joy in and at the Lord. Paul says, in verse **4**a, "Rejoice in the Lord..." In other words, "It's in the Lord where we have peace! It's in the Lord where we have liberty! It's in the Lord where we have joy!" Nehemiah said, "The joy of the Lord is my strength." In other words, Nehemiah said, "It's a great day in the Lord," because he had joy!

That's what we need to have as Christians! More joy! More joy in the right location of our hearts! More joy, not in our heads, but more joy in our hearts. Even the hardest of hearts need more joy!

Joy! Joy! Joy! Joy! Down in our hearts. Down in our hearts today! I'm so happy! So very happy, I have the love of Jesus in my heart! I have the love of Jesus in my heart!

Are you happy? So very happy, that you have the love of Jesus in your heart? Are you happy? So very happy, that you have the love of Jesus in your heart? We thirst for a spiritual awakening. More joy!

Second, it's a great day in the Lord when we set the right limitation that won't restrict or restrain our unconditional joy!

Paul said that there is no limit to the kind of joy we have in Jesus! The joy we have in Jesus is *always*! Paul said in Philippians **4:4**b, "*...always...*" And *always* means *always*. It means forever and ever and ever and ever! John **1:1** says, "In the beginning was the Word, and the Word was with God, and the Word was God." In other words, *always*!

Do not allow anything to limit your joy! Unlimited joy is like unlimited grace–it's amazing! "Amazing Grace, how sweet the sound that saved a wretch like me. I once was lost but now I'm found, was blind but now, I see!" Do you have unlimited, unrestricted joy? We desire a spiritual awakening! Unlimited, unrestrictive joy!

Third, it's a great day in the Lord when we establish the right lifestyle to continue our unconditional joy!

When we get to heaven, we are going to meet *joy* face to face. There will be a new heaven and a new earth. We shall be changed in the moment of a twinkle of an eye and we shall be like Him! That is why the Apostle Paul said it like this in Philippians **4:4**c: *"...I will say it again: Rejoice!"*

Does your joy have the right lifestyle? Not stylish joy, but lifestyle joy! A joy where in everything you do, you do it with joy! Joy! This joy I have–the world didn't give it and the world can't take it away! The Holy Ghost I have–the world didn't give it and the world can't take it away! Joy! Joy! Joy! We need the right kind of joy! We hunger for a spiritual awakening! Fashion for a righteous lifestyle!

It's a great day in the Lord! It's a great day in the Lord! Why? Because I have joy! I have unconditional joy and I can't help but rejoice anyway! Paul said, "Rejoice in the Lord, always and I will say it again: Rejoice!" I would like for each of us to do what the Word says, so in your own way, Rejoice!

Consider Calvary: It's a Great Day in the Lord–Rejoice!

It was out on a hill called Calvary where my joy was restored! "On a hill far away stood an old rugged cross, the emblem of suffering and shame, and I love that old cross was the dearest and best..." My unconditional joy was restored at the Cross! Now we are able to say unconditionally that "It's a great day in the Lord." Why? Because...

Our gentleness is evident to all. Now read prayerfully the results of a great day in the Lord. As you read, remember to employ both your head and your heart. Allow the Spirit of God to reveal to you what it means to preach the Good News of the gospel of Jesus Christ with a passionate desire for a Spiritual Awakening.

1. We know that the Lord is near
2. We are not anxious about anything
3. We are presenting everything to God in prayer and petition
4. We have thanksgiving in our heart
5. We have peace in our soul
6. We have understanding in our mind
7. We will have truth
8. We will have nobility

9. We will have rightness
10. We will have purity
11. We will have loveliness
12. We will have admiration
13. We will have excellence
14. We will have praiseworthiness
15. We will have learned knowledge
16. We will have received what God has for us
17. We will have received God's best
18. We will have heard the Good News
19. We will have put into practice what we have learned
20. We will have the God of peace with us always
21. We will have salvation and eternal life in joy!

Therefore, "It's a great day in the Lord!" So, rejoice in the Lord always. I will say it again: Rejoice! So, how long should a Christian rejoice? "Always!"

Embrace the Truth

Operating in the power of always, Jesus died! And joy showed up! They beat Him, but joy showed up! They mocked Him, but joy showed up! They placed Him in a borrowed tomb, but joy showed up! Then on that Easter Sunday morning, He got up with all joy in His hands–then joy graduated to rejoicing! Saints, rejoice in the Lord always. I will say it again: Rejoice!

What is your greatest joy? My greatest joy is my Salvation! Are you saved? If you are not, then you don't have joy! And if you don't have joy, then there will always be a battle going on between *Prosperous Fragrance* and *Pleasant Acquaintance* (your flesh and your faith). Settle the matter today and come to Jesus! Jesus died to set you free! He died on Calvary's tree just for you and me!

Exchange Your Sorrows for Great Joy

Come to Jesus while you have time and He will give you joy! As Christians, we must learn to live up to our name. As Christians, we boldly desire to experience what it means to say unapologetically, "It's a great day in the Lord!" Claim every word in this chapter and receive wholeheartedly what you have read in this chapter, now! Say aloud, deep within your soul, "Lord, send a revival! Lord, send a revival! Lord, send revival! And let it begin with me!" We need a spiritual awakening–filled with joy!

"It's a great day in the Lord–Rejoice!"

Chapter 11

David's Dream Team: David's Mighty Men

"These are the names of David's mighty men: Josheb-basshebeth, a Tahkemonite, was chief of the Three; he raised his spear against eight hundred men, whom he killed in one encounter."
2 SAMUEL **23:8**, NIV

In **2** Samuel **23:8**–ff., the Bible says, "These are the names of David's mighty men." Chapters 9 and 11 are similar in both substance and significance. David, son of Jesse, was in the early stages of his life, an innocent little shepherd boy, whereas, chapter 11 reports on King David in the later period of his life. David is now reaping what he has sown. God has forgiven David of all his sins, yet the fruit of his sins is now producing a major harvest of pain, suffering, shame, rebellion, suffering, and even death of his own sons.

I want you to be very mindful of what you are about to read. Like in chapter 9, "The Giant Killer" you will be tempted to rush through the chapter in order to get to the end. I would humbly say to you, "Don't take the short cut." There is a powerful message in these Scriptures designed for you to understand what it requires to not only be a mighty man of God like King David, but this also will help you learn how to identify the qualities in men who you will need to be on your team of mighty men of God.

So, don't rush through this chapter. I realize that if you have been in ministry for a number of years that you will be tempted to say, "I've read this passage several times. What can I learn from reading this same old passage again?" I have learned that you can read the same passage a dozen times in one day and the Holy Spirit of God will impart new insights and illuminations on each occasion. Therefore, read the entire chapter from start to finish. The reward comes in the end. I have learned to read and re-read what I have read time after time after time, and each time God speaks to me in a new and fresh way. Take a moment and go back to chapters 2 and 3 in this book and you will see exactly what I mean. Chapters 2 and 3 are essentially written from the same Scripture passage. However, chapter 3 was written years after the other. Chapter 2 was written and rewritten numerous times. I have taught on both chapters, however chapter 2 addresses the inner life of the believer. Chapter 3 boldly declares that when a church or a people neglect to embrace the holiness of God, that church or people is in grave danger.

I want to say it one more time, read this chapter for all its worth. I am sure God will open your eyes to see things that even I have not written on these pages. Read the Scripture. Read it from start to finish. I assure you God will honor your effort. I would suggest as you read the foundation passage that you simply read and reflect on both the subheadings and the substance of the Scripture passage. Later, I will expound in more detail as it relates to what certain names mean in the full scheme of the biblical story of David's Dream Team: David's Mighty Men.

• Josheb-basshebeth–Chief of the Three Mighty Men

Josheb-basshebeth, a Tahkemonite, was chief of the Three; he raised his spear against eight hundred men, whom he killed in one encounter.

• Eleazar the Ahohite–Stood His Ground

Next to him was Eleazar son of Dodai the Ahohite. As one of the three mighty men, he was with David when they taunted the Philistines gathered [at Pas Dammim] for battle. Then the men of Israel retreated, but he stood his ground and struck down the Philistines till his hand grew tired and froze to the sword. The Lord brought about a great victory that day. The troops returned to Eleazar, but only to strip the dead.

• Shammah the Hararite–Took His Stand

Next to him was Shammah son of Agee the Hararite. When the Philistines banded together at a place where there was a field full of lentils, Israel's troops fled from them. But Shammah took his stand in the middle of the field. He defended it and struck the Philistines down, and the Lord brought about a great victory.

• David's Stronghold–The Cave of Adullam

During harvest time, three of the thirty chief men came down to David at the cave of Adullam, while a band of Philistines was encamped in the Valley of Rephaim. At that time David was in the stronghold, and the Philistine garrison was at Bethlehem. David longed for water and said, "Oh, that someone would get me a drink of water from the well near the gate of Bethlehem!" So the three mighty men broke through the Philistine lines, drew water from the well near the gate of Bethlehem and carried it back to David. But he refused to drink it; instead, he poured it out before the Lord. "Far be it from me, O Lord, to do this!" he said. "Is it not the blood of men who went at the risk of their lives?" And David would not drink it. Such were the exploits of the three mighty men.

• Abishai–Killed Three Hundred Men with His Spear

Abishai the brother of Joab son of Zeruiah was chief of the Three. He raised his spear against three hundred men, whom he killed, and so he became as famous as the Three. Was he not held in greater honor than the Three? He became their commander, even though he was not included among them.

• Benaiah–Killed a Lion Down in a Pit on a Snowy Day

Benaiah son of Jehoiada was a valiant fighter from Kabzeel, who performed great exploits. He struck down two of Moab's best men. He also went down into a pit on a snowy day and killed a lion. And he struck down a huge Egyptian. Although the Egyptian had a spear in his hand, Benaiah went against him with a club. He snatched the spear from the Egyptian's hand and killed him with his own spear. Such were the exploits of Benaiah son of Jehoiada; he too was as famous as the three mighty men. He was held in greater honor than any of the Thirty, but he was not included among the Three. And David put him in charge of his bodyguard.

2 SAMUEL **23:8-23**, NIV

The heart and soul of a mighty man of God! David's Dream Team: David's Mighty Men.

Five Mighty Men

According to the Word of God, man is a trichotomy: First, man is body. Second, man is soul. Third, man is spirit. In other words, man has a body, a soul and a spirit. First, as a body, man is a physical manifestation of God's divine creation! Second, as a soul, man is an inner manifestation of God's unique creation! Third, as a spirit, man is an eternal manifestation of God's providential creation! So, man is physical, man is inner, and man is eternal. This is the heart and soul of a Mighty Man of God!

In 2 Samuel Chapter 23, the Bible gives us the five mightiest of the mighty men in our story and these brothers are the five baddest, boldest, bravest brothers in the house. These five brothers aren't afraid of anybody. These five brothers are not afraid of a good fight and these five brothers are like mighty weapons in the hands of King David–to help King David secure his kingdom from the enemies outside of the camp of God and from the enemies entrenched within the camp of God. That is why the Bible says that these five brothers were the five baddest, boldest, bravest brothers in town!

The Five Mighty Men

1) Josheb-Basshebeth, a Tahkemonite–The word *Tahkemonite* means "Thou will make me wise." Therefore, Josheb-Basshebeth was a man of profound wisdom. He was chief of David's Three (2 Sam. 23:8).[1]

2) Eleazer, son of Dodai the Ahohite–The word *Eleazer* means "God has helped." The name *Dodai* means "his beloved." The name *Ahohite* means "brother of rest, or frat brother or each for the other." Therefore, Eleazer was a man who "God had helped to help others help themselves." He was one of David's three mighty men who helped in his battle against the Philistines (2 Sam. 23:9; 1 Chr. 11:12).[2]

3) Shammah, son of Agee the Hararite–The word *Shammah* means "to be desolate." The word *Agee* means "I shall increase." The word *Hararite* means "mountain dweller." Therefore, Shammah was a man who God had increased, despite the fact that he had encountered some desolate times" (2

---

1 David Noel Freedman, *Eerdmans Dictionary of the Bible*, 737
2 Ibid., 389.

Sam. **23:11–12, 33**; cf. **1** Chr. **11:34**).[3]

4) Abishai, the brother of Joab, son of Zeruiah–The word *Abishai* means "my father is a gift." The word *Joab* means "Jehovah is Father." The name *Zeruiah* means "balsam or salve." Therefore, Abishai was a man who Jehovah God the Father used as a gift who was the son of "healing." He was a gifted healer or deliverer of God's people. "Within David's administration, he appears as a kind of second-in-command of the army, and he is typical of David's inner circle of advisors with his combination of loyalty to, yet independence from, the king."[4]

5) Benaiah, son of Jehoiada from Kabzeel–The word *Benaiah* means "Jehovah has built." The word *Jehoiada* means "Jehovah knows." The word *Kabzeel* means "God gathers." Therefore, Benaiah was a man whom Jehovah God had built and Jehovah God knew personally for Himself that Benaiah was totally committed toward "being a gatherer of people" for God's glory! His deeds were renowned among David's Thirty, although he was not part of the Three (**2** Sam. **23:20–23**; **1** Chr. **11:22-25**). He was close to David even at his death. He helped David's son, Solomon, secure his kingdom following the death of his dad. Benaiah killed Adonijah (**1** Kgs. **2:25**), Joah (vv. **29-34**), and Shimei (v. **46**). Solomon rewarded Benaiah by placing him over all the army instead of Joab (**1** Kgs. **2:35**). He had been over David's militia of twenty-four thousand, which served during the third month. He was indeed a mighty man.[5]

Five Mighty Weapons

David's dream team: David's mighty men, had five weapons that every mighty man of God has available at his fingertips! The weapons are:

1. The weapon of godly Leadership
2. The weapon of godly Perseverance
3. The weapon of godly Courage

3 Ibid., 1196.
4 Ibid., 8.
5 Ibid., 164.

4. The weapon of godly Character

5. The weapon of godly Determination

In order to understand David's plight, we must examine each of these weapons in the hands of David's most trusted mighty men.

1. The weapon of Godly Leadership

This weapon was in the hand of Josheb-Basshebeth, a Tahkemonite. He clearly possessed the weapon of godly Leadership. He was a man of wisdom. His name bears witness of the fact. His name meant "Thou will make me wise." The report on Josheb-Basshebeth, a Tahkemonite, was saturated with deep insight–the kind of insight David greatly needed around him, given the fact that David was in constant danger of losing his leadership as King of Israel. David was often on the run like when he was hiding in the Cave of Adullam with his band of mighty men.

However, to make matters worse, David was told by God that he would be king, but King Saul did not want to relinquish the throne. This truly complicated the matter of who was really in charge. The truth of the matter was that God was in charge. Whether we want it or not, God is always in charge. He is always in control. When we think things are out of control, God is still on top of His game.

Bret Favre, Hall of Fame quarterback for the Green Bay Packers, was eventually released from the team. Favre decided he would retire, but something deep within him did not retire. Bret Favre decided to play one more season. And as fate would have it, he was picked up by the Minnesota Vikings. Once again, Bret Favre became the number one quarterback in the National Football League (NFL).

The Green Bay Packers concluded that he was finished, washed up, but he was not. This is the same way it is with God. God is never washed up. He is never finished. He can use whoever He desires to achieve His ultimate purpose and that is to save His people. Luke **19:10** says, "for the Son of Man has come to seek and to save that which was lost." The Lord filled Josheb-Basshebeth, a Tahkemonite, with wisdom to help David establish his kingdom.

We should never lose faith in God. God will never let us down. That is why it is not just good to be on David's dream team, but it is far better to be on the Lord's dream team of eternal wisdom and success. Wisdom is always on time.

2. The weapon of Godly Perseverance

Here is the report on Eleazer, the son of Dodai the Ahohite. He possessed the weapon of godly Perseverance. David was, once again, running for his life. He not only needed a mighty man of wisdom, he needed a mighty man of perseverance. He needed a man who had the inherent ability that refused to quit.

Yet, he was still just a man. David was running for his life and Eleazer was on the run with him. Just because he was on the run it did not mean that he was afraid to fight. Eleazer did not allow fear to contaminate his faith in Almighty God and his beloved king, David.

Eleazer found great peace in knowing that he was a man who refused to give up when the going got tough and the hills were hard to climb. Eleazer was like the song we sang many years ago titled "I've Decided to Make Jesus My Choice." Whenever we make Jesus our choice, we have already won. We are indeed victorious. As long as Jesus is in control, we have the victory. This ought to make us stop and praise the Lord for He is worthy of all our praise. The Psalmist declared in the Psalter, in Psalm 150:1, "Praise the Lord, Praise God in His sanctuary." Our God desires all the praise. For this is the day the Lord has made, let us rejoice and be glad in it. As you read each report on David's Dream Team: David's Mighty Men, ask the Lord to bless your ministry with godly men to help you come out of your cave of Adullam and take authority over the worldly influences of the day.

• Eleazar–Mighty Man of Godly Perseverance

Next to him was Eleazar son of Dodai the Ahohite. As one of the three mighty men, he was with David when they taunted the Philistines gathered [at Pas Dammim] for battle. Then the men of Israel retreated, but he stood his ground and struck down the Philistines till his hand grew tired and froze to the sword. The Lord brought about a great victory that day. The troops returned to Eleazar, but only to strip the dead.

2 SAMUEL 23:9-10, NIV

3. The weapon of Godly Courage

The third mighty man of the five men to report on is Shammah, son of Agee the Hararite. According to tradition, it is said that he possessed the weapon of Godly Courage. Given the climate and condition of David's situation, he needed a man who possessed the innate ability of courage. Shammah was not afraid of anybody or anything. He was one of David's most trusted mighty men.

Yet, what made matters worse, King Saul did not care what his name stood for or meant. King Saul simply wanted to kill David and all his mighty men. But God would not allow this to happen. We do not ever have to worry when we are working for the Lord. When the Lord is on our side and He is clearly with us, we are able to rest our confidence on this Biblical truth: "He who is in you is greater than he who is in the world" (1 John 4:4). God is truly greater than any and everything we could ever come face to face with on our life's journey to wholeness and holiness, fasting and prayer.

Mark Chapter 9 reveals the story of the little boy who was demon possessed. In chapter one of this book, I shared with you how this little boy received his healing. The Bible said, "Jesus healed him." But what did Jesus tell His disciples, who did all they could do, yet they failed in performing this miracle? Jesus told His disciples that they forgot one thing: "This kind can come out by nothing but prayer and fasting" (Mark 9:29). In other words, God is our ultimate Deliverer. God sent King David the help he needed. The Bible says:

• Shammah: Mighty Man of Godly Courage

Next to him was Shammah son of Agee the Hararite. When the Philistines banded together at a place where there was a field full of lentils, Israel's troops fled from them. But Shammah took his stand in the middle of the field. He defended it and struck the Philistines down, and the Lord brought about a great victory.
2 SAMUEL 23:11-12, NIV

4. The weapon of Godly Character

The fourth weapon David had in his possession came in the person of Abishai, the brother of Joab, son of Zeruiah. The report on Abishai was an insightful one. The word *Abishai* means "my father is a gift." The word *Joab* means "Jehovah is Father." The name *Zeruiah* means balsam or salve." Therefore, Abishai was a man who Jehovah used to heal the wounds of men, particularly his trusted leader and king, David.

There is no need to run, when you have healing support on your mighty men's dream team. But there were times that David was running so hard, he literally forgot what God had provided for his defense.

Like David, we as Christians at war on the battlefield for the Lord, must never forget Who is with us. We have the Lord on our side. We cannot fail.

God is with us. Paul said, in Romans **8:28**, "And we know that all things work together for good to those who love God, to those who are the called according to His purpose." Furthermore in Romans **8:37**, Paul says, "we are more than conquerors through Him who loved us."

To put it bluntly, we are somebody. So, why don't we start acting like we are somebody in the Lord? Let the world know we are the King's kids. We are somebody. Praise the Lord. The Bible says:

• Abishai–Mighty Man of Godly Character

Abishai the brother of Joab son of Zeruiah was chief of the Three. He raised his spear against three hundred men, whom he killed, and so he became as famous as the Three. Was he not held in greater honor than the Three? He became their commander, even though he was not included among them.
2 SAMUEL **23:18-19**, NIV

5. The weapon of Godly Determination

Now, there was one more mighty man of the five. His name was Benaiah, son of Jehoiada from Kabzeel. The report on Benaiah was transformational for any preacher who is seeking to preach for spiritual awakening and revival. The word *Benaiah* means "Jehovah has built." The word *Jehoiada* means "Jehovah knows." The word *Kabzeel* means "God gathers."

Benaiah was ready for the task. He was ready, willing, and able to defend his king, David, from the evil attacks of King Saul and others. Although he was ready, it did not mean that he did not have to retreat from time to time in order to reposition himself for the greater battle.

In order to restore order to one's life, there comes a time and a season where we need to pull back, regroup, reestablish, and recalculate our strategy. Why? It is necessary to be able to see the whole picture. That is why Benaiah, son of Jehoiada's from Kabzeel name implied "one who Jehovah knows."

As long as we know that God knows, then we can rest assured that, in due season, He will let us know, as well. But, even if He does not, we will still trust Him anyway. That is exactly what Benaiah did. He trusted in what the Lord knew.

When we do this, we will develop a peace which passes all understanding. This is the type of peace that is available to all of us as God's elect–His chosen people. In **1** Peter **2:9**, the Bible says, "But you are a chosen generation, a royal priesthood, a holy nation, His own special people, that you may proclaim the praises of Him who called you out of darkness into His marvelous light."

We are somebody. Tell the world that we are children of the Most High God. We are somebody. That's why we ought to praise His Holy and Righteous Name–The Name is Jesus!

This is David's dream team: David's mighty men. So, Benaiah son of Jehoiada from Kabzeel, he possessed the weapon of godly determination.

• Benaiah –Mighty Man of Godly Determination

Benaiah son of Jehoiada was a valiant fighter from Kabzeel, who performed great exploits. He struck down two of Moab's best men. He also went down into a pit on a snowy day and killed a lion. And he struck down a huge Egyptian. Although the Egyptian had a spear in his hand, Benaiah went against him with a club. He snatched the spear from the Egyptian's hand and killed him with his own spear. Such were the exploits of Benaiah son of Jehoiada; he too was as famous as the three mighty men. He was held in greater honor than any of the Thirty, but he was not included among the Three. And David put him in charge of his bodyguard.

2 Samuel **23:20-23**, NIV

But what was it that made these men the mightiest of the Mighty Men Of God in the camp of God?

First, they knew who they were. Second, they were not afraid of their enemies. Third, they were not afraid of accepting heavy responsibilities. In the same way, this ought to be us.

I have been told that Detroit was known as "the Motor City Capital of the World." What would happen if Detroit became known as "The Mighty Men of God Capital of the World"? Better still. What would happen if your church became known as "the Mighty Men's Capital of _____?" And better than that: What if you were called "the Mightiest of all the Mighty Men in your church?" If I told you how you can become a man like this, would you respond?

Take the next step now. What an incredible resource in the hands of God to bring spiritual awakening. Imagine all the men and women in your church being totally surrendered to God. Could God bring revival and spiritual awakening to our nation through people who know who they are, are not afraid of their enemies, and are not afraid of accepting heavy responsibilities? There is no doubt that God could!

Chapter 12
My God, My God, Why?

From the sixth hour until the ninth hour darkness came over all the land. About the ninth hour Jesus cried out in a loud voice, "Eloi, Eloi, lama sabachthani?"–which means, "My God, my God, why have you forsaken me?"
MATTHEW **27:45-46**, NIV

There comes a time in the life of every man, woman, boy or girl, when you are perplexed and propelled to cry out of the midst of your personal pain and uttermost agony and frustration: "Why? Why, God? Why?" Then you sigh, "Lord. Why are you doing this to me? What have I done so bad to experience so much pain? Lord. Why are you doing this to me?"

In the same way, Jesus Christ, God's only begotten Son (John **3:16**, KJV) was confronted with an even more perplexing encounter. This moment in time stunned Jesus Christ, the Son of Man, yet emboldened Jesus Christ, the Son of God. Therefore, let us explore the place where He was approaching His final days, known as the Week of Passion.

In Matthew Chapter **21:1-11**, Jesus makes His triumphant entrance into the city of Jerusalem. It is Palm Sunday. Excitement is in the air. The disciples eagerly went and did as Jesus had instructed them to do. Filled with expectancy, they brought the donkey and the colt and placed their garments on the back of them. Jesus then sat upon them and rode into the city of Jerusalem.

Crowds spilled over into the streets, as they placed their cloaks on the dusty road, while countless others cut branches and spread them on the road on which Jesus traveled. In the heat of excitement, palm branches were exuberantly scattered in the streets as Christ came riding into the city of Jerusalem. Then without prompting, the crowds of people followed Him as they shouted, "Hosanna to the Son of David! Blessed is He who comes in the name of the Lord! Hosanna in the highest!"

On Monday, Jesus cursed a barren fig tree (Matt. **21:18-22**). An unknown, scholar suggested that the curse of the barren fig tree illustrates the spiritual condition of the people of God. While another writer suggests that Jesus is attempting to teach His disciples a lesson on the power of prayer and the usefulness of doubtless faith (Matt. **21:21**).

On Tuesday and Wednesday, Jesus told four stirring parables.[1] He employed parables to help His listeners discover the mysteries of heaven while on earth.

On Thursday, Jesus transitioned the Passover Meal of the Old Testament to the Lord's Supper to communicate a picture of grace over law (Matt. **26:17-20; 26:26-29**). However, Jesus is betrayed by Judas Iscariot for thirty pieces of silver to the Roman authorities (Matt. **26:47-56**). Jesus is now ready to surrender His life for our death. Here He will soon become our perfect sacrifice by placing on Himself the sins of the world. Isaiah **53:4**, says, "Surely He has borne our griefs and carried our sorrows; yet we esteemed Him stricken, smitten by God, and afflicted." He did what no man could do to save us from our sin. Paul reports, in Roman **6:23**, "For the wages of sin is death, but the gift of God is eternal life in Christ Jesus our Lord."

It's Good Friday and the enemy (i.e., death) is literally knocking at the door of God's Son. Jesus is now before the High Priest, Caiaphas (Matt. **26:57**). His days on earth are fast eroding. All the powers of Rome, the religious establishment of Israel, and the crowds of the people that once celebrated Him were eager to see Him crucified. Other than His heavenly Father, all Jesus has left to comfort Him was his most trusted disciple. Time will unveil the measure of the faith and commitment of His closest disciple Simon Peter, the rock, His right hand man.

Like all the others who were with Jesus in His years of inauguration and popularity, Jesus is now blatantly denied to His face by Peter three consecutive times then the cock crows his final time (Matt. **26:58, 69-75**). Peter is pierced to the heart by the dagger of shame. He did what he never thought he would do. Deny his Master, Christ.

Now, Judas is shaken to the core of his soul. In an effort to redeem himself, he attempts to return the thirty pieces of silver he was paid for betraying Christ and the Roman authorities refused to accept his plea. In utter guilt of the crime he committed, Judas goes out and hangs himself (Matt. **27:3-10**). Judas is dead.

---

1 The five parables are as follows: The Parable of the Two Sons (Matt. 21:28-32), The Parable of the Wicked Husbandman (Matt. 21:22-41), The Parable of the King's Son (Matt. 22:1-14), The Parable of the Ten Virgins (Matt. 25:1-13), and The Parable of the Ten Talents (Matt. 25:14-30).

Jesus is now being led away to the cross, Via Dolorosa (Matt. **27:31-33**). As Christ comes to the place of skulls, Golgotha, for His crucifixion, they raise Him up between two thieves (Matt. **27:35-38**). His garments are gambled away (John **19:23-24**). He is mocked as the King of Jews (Matt. **27:39-43**), even while giving His life for the sins of the world. He forgives the thief on cross hanging at His right side, and then He commends His mother to John (Luke **23:39-43**; John **19:25-27**). As darkness looms over the earth like the deepest and darkness of all midnights, Jesus cries out in a loud voice. "Eloi, Eloi, lama sabachthani?" which means, "My God, my God, why have You forsaken me?" (Matt **27:45-50**). Then He pants, "I thirst" (John **19:28**). "It is finished," He says (John **19:30**). "Father, into thy hands I commend my spirit" (Luke **23:46**). Jesus is dead.

As for me, each and every word of Christ echoes deep within the chambers of my soul. However, I pray what I am sharing with you will awaken something deep within you as it has done for me. It happens when one knows not what to do. It is that period of time between life and death. Jesus says, it best, "My God, My God. Why?" (Matt. **27:46**).

Five Key Words

These were five words that changed the face of history. My life was changed by these five, yet powerful, transformation words. Something within my inner being was stimulated. One might say, I was not simply aroused, I was awakening by the power of the Holy Spirit of God to see my suffering and pain in a completely different way. Initially, I had concluded that pain and suffering must be avoided.

Countless physicians make a vibrant living prescribing medicine and expensive treatment in assisting their clients in pain management. A number of people I know deal with pain on a daily basis. Some live a life of pain practically moment by moment. Prior to allowing God help me unpack the essence of the Passion of the Christ, I considered pain as something to be avoided like a plague. However, I failed to realize the gift of pain and suffering.

Pain and suffering answers the question why. The question why always addresses the concept of reason. Why is this like this? Why this and not that? Why me and why not her? Why is the question that probes to unearth the undercurrents of reason? Particularly, reason that is situated in two domains. The first domain is the theologically and second one is the epistemologically domain.

In presenting this study on *Preaching for Spiritual Awakening*, I want to challenge you, the reader, not to flee from the gifts of pain and suffering. When you are willing to endure the pain, the shame, and the humiliation of your personal crucifixion, you will come out on the other side of your individual resurrection. Now stop and think of the kind of Spiritual power you will possess. Like Christ, you will receive power when the Holy Spirit comes on you and you will tell others just like I'm telling you (Acts 1:4-8).

So, hang in there and don't come down from your cross. Why? Simple! After you have completed your battle with your cross, and you have been placed in your assigned tomb, just like Jesus, you better get ready for a major change. But, don't get in too big of a hurry, you've got to die and you've got to be buried. Listen to the words of the Apostle Matthew as he testifies concerning the death, burial, and resurrection of the Lord Jesus Christ.

Immediately, in Matthew 27:57-61, the Scriptures report of a rich man from Arimathea named Joseph, who himself had also become a disciple of Jesus." He boldly moved to bury Jesus. There was no record of the other disciples participating in burying the Lord. Joseph evidentially was not only rich financially but he was rich spiritually. True wealth is never measured by man's standard. God measures the wealth of the heart over against the wealth of material possessions.

Read what Joseph did. Read not simply to understand words on a page but read to discern the work of the Holy Spirit of God who enables us to preach for deep spiritual change in the lives of the sheep God has placed under our leadership. The question that continues to haunt me is this. Where were the disciples? Where were those of the inner circle–Peter, James, and John? Were they hiding in fear of losing their lives? Why didn't they come to help bury their Master Teacher?

As you read word for word the account of the burial of Jesus, I would like you to ask yourself a few questions. The first question is this. Would you have helped Joseph of Arimathea? Second, when you are going through hard times, are there people in your congregation you can depend on to help you? Finally, why do you preach the Word of God? Do you preach God's Word for filthy lucre? Are you a man of moral principle or are you a man of personal gain? As you read this account, stop and pray for yourself. Pray that you will preach for spiritual awakening with passion, power, promise, and perfect peace in Jesus Christ–the Prince of Peace.

Now when evening had come, there came a rich man from Arimathea, named Joseph, who himself had also become a disciple of Jesus. This man went to Pilate and asked for the body of Jesus. Then Pilate commanded the body to be given to him. When Joseph had taken the body, he wrapped it in a clean linen cloth, and laid it in his new tomb which he had hewn out of the rock; and he rolled a large stone against the door of the tomb, and departed. And Mary Magdalene was there, and the other Mary, sitting opposite the tomb.

MATTHEW **27:57-61**

What do you think about what you have just read? You don't have to tell anyone. God already knows what is within your heart. He know why you do what you do. He knows the mind and motives of all men. "Nothing in all creation is hidden from God's sight. Everything is uncovered and laid bare before the eyes of him to whom we must give account" (Heb. **4:13**). Did you read and meditate on Matthew **27:57-61**? If you did, then God bless you. If you did not, then I want to ask you a few questions. Why didn't you? Have you already read it before and you felt it was not necessary to read it again? My brother, if you have not read Matthew **27:57-61**, back up and do it immediately.

Jesus is now dead, just like you may be dead in your ministry or your service to the Lord. You may have had all the life sucked out of you. Is it possible that you may be a dead man, walking around like a zombie? Jesus is in the tomb. Are you in your tomb? Be honest! Are you? Are you feeling dead and dried up? Are you ready to quit? Have you been placed in a tomb by someone you once knew? Jesus knew Nicodemus. It is not certain whether Jesus knew Joseph of Arimathea. Despite your present situation, in Matthew **27:59-60**, the Bible says: "When Joseph had taken the body, he wrapped it in a clean linen cloth, and laid it in his new tomb which he had hewn out of the rock; and he rolled a large stone against the door of the tomb, and departed."

"My God, My God, Why?" Why would God allow His Only Begotten Son to die for sinful man? Why would God literally turn His back on His One and Only Son? Would you do this for people who didn't love you? Would you do this for people who spat on you? Would you do this for folks who lied about you? Would you do this for all the sins of the world? "My God; My God; Why have you forsaken me?" Literally, the word forsaken is from the Greek New Testament word *egkale*.[2] *Egkale* means "to bring a charge against me," or "to

---

2 *Greek New Testament.*

accuse me," or "to institute judicial proceeding," or "to call me a common criminal."[3] "My God, My God, Why have you forsaken me?"

Are you wondering why your preaching is so dry? Why is your spiritual power zapped? Why are the people you miniser to uninterested, unenthusiastic, and unconcerned? Why is there little to no Spirit Power in your preaching and teaching of the Word of God? Have you ever said, "My God, My God, Why?"

The reason why is simple: God needed a spotless lamb for man's bond. There are times when God needs you and me to suffer and experience a painful cross in order to advance the work of the Kingdom of God. We must never forget that there is a difference in a test and a trial (James 1:2-3). The reason God sent Jesus the way of the cross is because man needed a Savior and Jesus was the answer. So what did Jesus do?

- First—Jesus died to set us from free from death, hell, and the grave. Remember this. When God sets us free, we are able to help free others.

    John 8:36, "Therefore if the Son makes you free, you shall be free indeed."

- Second—Jesus died to prepare a place for us. In the same way we cannot lead where we have not been. How can we prepare the way for others when we are not prepared ourselves? *Preaching for Spiritual Awakening* is about preaching with such confidence until people are compelled to follow us as we follow Christ.

    John 14:2b-3, "I go to prepare a place for you. And if I go and prepare a place for you, I will come again and receive you to Myself; that where I am, there you may be also."

- Third—Jesus died that we might be with Him in Paradise. The bridge across the turbulent waters of suffering, pain, and death is the cross. Neither you nor I can cross over without a cross. No cross. No cross. Like the thief, our crossing can be right now. Only if you Preach It! Brother! Preach the Word!

    Jesus said, in Luke 23:43, to the thief on the cross, "And Jesus said to him, 'Assuredly, I say to you, today you will be with Me in Paradise.'"

---

3 Ibid.

- Fourth—Jesus died so that we may evangelize others to know Jesus, too. Like Jesus, we need to remember that Pentecost is simply one step of obedience away. Christ died so that we might have Spirit Power. We serve others believing that we will encourage them to embrace and be endued with Spirit Power. Where there is Spirit Power, a genuine Spiritual Awakening is one step away. Will you take that step? Are you ready? If you are, take Jesus at His word.

Jesus said, in Acts 1:8, "But you shall receive power when the Holy Spirit has come upon you; and you shall be witnesses to Me in Jerusalem, and in all Judea and Samaria, and to the end of the earth."

- Finally—Jesus died to say to us that if we want to live, we too must die. Spiritual Awakening comes only after one is awakening to the supernatural things of God. Paul understood this. Listen to what Paul the apostle to the Gentiles declares.

In Galatians 2:20, the Bible says, "I have been crucified with Christ; it is no longer I who live, but Christ lives in me; and the life which I now live in the flesh I live by faith in the Son of God, who loved me and gave Himself for me."

Like both Paul and Jesus, you and I must first die to self. Why is it so difficult for us to die to self? I submit that there is a massive stone obstructing us. This massive stone is keeping us sealed in the tombs of our life circumstances. However, today, I want you to know that if you really know Jesus, "He Still Moves Stones!" "My God, My God, Why?" The answer is simple: "He Still Moves Stones." Stones blocking our growth, our peace, our joy, our finances, our faith, our freedom, our life, our dreams, and our hopes can be moved." I want you to know today that "God Still Moves Stones." My God, my God, why?...to move all the stones in our lives.

Is there anybody in the house today who can join in thanking Him? Is there anybody in the house today who can join me in celebrating what He has done for you? "My God, my God, why?" But, everybody doesn't know why? Because sin has separated them from the love of God, but you don't have to remain separated from the love of Christ. We can conqueror this thing!

Read and examine what Paul said concerning the things we are capable of knowing. Paul invites us to view our circumstances through the lens of our heavenly Father. As you study Paul's message to us as believers, count the number of times the name God is either explicit or implicit. Then, prayerfully identify what happened when God showed up in the passage of Scripture. Paul said,

• Section 1

And we know that in all things God works for the good of those who love Him, who have been called according to His purpose. For those God foreknew He also predestined to be conformed to the likeness of His Son, that He might be the firstborn among many brothers. And those He predestined, He also called; those He called, He also justified; those He justified, He also glorified. What, then, shall we say in response to this? If God is for us, who can be against us? He who did not spare His own Son, but gave Him up for us all—how will He not also, along with Him, graciously give us all things? Who will bring any charge against those whom God has chosen? It is God who justifies. Who is He that condemns? Christ Jesus, who died—more than that, who was raised to life—is at the right hand of God and is also interceding for us.

You have now prayerfully read Section 1 of Paul's message. Now, I would like for you to read Section 2. In reading Section 2 underscore or write on a note pad the number of times a question was raised. Now go back to Section 1 and on that same note pad jot down the number of times a question was raised. Then compare Section 1 with Section 2. Finally, answer this last question. What did the Lord reveal to you?

• Section 2

Who shall separate us from the love of Christ? Shall trouble or hardship or persecution or famine or nakedness or danger or sword? As it is written: "For your sake we face death all day long; we are considered as sheep to be slaughtered." No, in all these things we are more than conquerors through him who loved us. For I am convinced that neither death nor life, neither angels nor demons, neither the present nor the future, nor any powers, neither height nor depth, nor anything else in all creation, will be able to separate us from the love of God that is in Christ Jesus our Lord.
ROMANS **8:28-39**, NIV

What is the solution? The solution is Preaching Jesus! He is the Savior of the world. I want you to be honest. Did He die for you? Is He your Savior? Is

He your Lord? Do you really know Him? If you don't know Him, you need to get to know Him right now! Now is the time! Now is the day for salvation! Come to Jesus! Why? He came to us to save us from our sins. Jesus laid down His life so that we might have hope in the midst of hopeless. He is our blessed hope. He is our redemptive hope. He is our heavenly hope. We have hope. Jesus is our eternal hope. Now we can make it. We have no reason to fret. Jesus once crucified, now alive forevermore.

Possibly consumed by the passion of the Christ and power of the Spirit of God which ushers in the revival and awakening to the human soul, George Bennard penned these words in 1913.

> On a hill far away stood an old rugged cross, the emblem of suff'ring and shame; and I love that old cross where the dearest and best for a world of lost sinners was slain. So I'll cherish the old rugged cross, till my trophies at last I lay down; I will cling to the old rugged cross, And exchange it someday for a crown.

"My God, My God, Why?" My answer to this question is this. Why not? I can't do enough to expression my love to Christ. Isaiah **6:8** said, "Here am I. Send me!"

Chapter 13

We Need to Practice What We Preach

The teachers of the law and the Pharisees sit in Moses' seat. So you must obey them and do everything they tell you. But do not do what they do, for they do not practice what they preach.
MATTHEW **23:2-3**, NIV

If we don't practice it, then we don't need to preach it. We need to do what we say that we are going to do, and just do it. Do it even if no one sees you doing what you're supposed to do. God sees what we are doing. Don't talk it if we are not walking it. Talk is cheap. We need to learn how to spend less time talking about what we are going to do and just do it. In other words, we need to practice what we preach.

Jesus was in His final week of ministry here on earth. He was on His way to the cross, but He had some unfinished business. He wanted to warn the crowds that were following Him and His disciples about the toxic teaching of the teachers of the law and the pompous parading of the hypocritical, prideful Pharisees. Reading and applying this passage will be easy for some but very difficult for others. It all depends on one's perspective of how we view ourselves. I view myself as one whom God has saved from my sins and engrafted me into the true vine of eternal life. I am a Christian. I am born again, however, I still reside in the body. I can be pious, self-righteous, egocentric, and prideful all it the same time.

I am not sure as to how you view yourself, but I pray your view is from Scripture. If not this is going to be either a painful passage or a passage in which you will be able to see the sinful faults of others. As your read, first re-examine your view of Scripture, then read with God's view as opposed to your own. The Bible says:

Then Jesus said to the crowds and to His disciples: "The teachers of the law and the Pharisees sit in Moses' seat. So you must obey them and do everything they tell you. But do not do what they do, for they do not practice what they preach. They tie up heavy loads and put them on men's shoulders, but they themselves are not willing to lift a finger to move them."

MATTHEW 23:1-4, NIV

The teachers of the law and the Pharisees were very religious, but they did not practice what they preached. Do you practice what you preach? Or do you challenge others to do as you say? I realize this is hard saying. I am not trying to embarrass anyone. I simply want to make my case clear. I don't want anyone to read this chapter and walk away and say, "He wasn't talking to me." In the same way, I don't want anyone to read the Word and say, "He's trying to convict me." Convict is not my job. Convict is the work of the Holy Spirit of God. He, the Holy Spirit, brings conviction. Read and ask God to help you understand a passage you may have read before. However this time allow the passage to read you. Jesus said:

"Everything they do is done for men to see: They make their phylacteries wide and the tassels on their garments long; they love the place of honor at banquets and the most important seats in the synagogues; they love to be greeted in the marketplaces and to have men call them 'Rabbi.' "

MATTHEW 23:5-7, NIV

God does not want us to do what these people did–practicing for the approval of man. This is not the solution to "Practicing What We Preach." So what is the solution to the problem when it comes to us practicing what we preach? How do we really become great in the eyes of God?

Jesus made two key statements that give us direction for practicing what you preach. First, He said, "The teachers of the law and the Pharisees sit in Moses' seat. So you must obey them and do everything they tell you. But do not do what they do, for they do not practice what they preach" (Matt. 23:2-3, NIV). Second, Jesus said, "The greatest among you will be your servant. For whoever exalts himself will be humbled, and whoever humbles himself will be exalted" (Matt. 23:11-12, NIV).

What keeps believers from practicing what they preach? Jesus made it clear that we are not to be like the Pharisees and we are to be like a servant who humbles himself. Are there some reasons as to why we won't humble ourselves and simply serve God and each other? If you do not understand what you turn to that is wrong, then your actions will never be corrected. So, let us examine some of the reasons why we don't practice what we preach.

7 Reasons For Not Practicing What We Preach

1. A **hindrance** will keep us from practicing what we preach.

> A hindrance is anything that stands between you and God. It is that which even Christians exalt above the throne of grace and mercy. That's a hindrance. I wonder, do you have anything standing between you and God? If you do, that is your hindrance. You need to get rid of it now. If not, then listen to the preaching of Jesus. In Matthew **23**:**13** (NIV), Jesus says, "Woe to you, teachers of the law and Pharisees, you hypocrites! You shut the kingdom of heaven in men's faces. You yourselves do not enter, nor will you let those enter who are trying to."

2. Is it possible that we **don't truly love God** more than we love the things of the world?

> When we elevate the things of the world, such as our money, our material possessions, our educations, and our careers; then we are revealing our love for self over our love for the Savior–the Lord Jesus Christ. Should I continue in sin that the grace of God abound or continue in sin? In others words, if we think God is going to save us from hell, yet we blatantly live as if we want to spend eternity in hell, then God will not give up on us. His permissive will allows us the free will to say no to Him. This is not His choice, it is our desire. God will not force His perfect will (i.e., what He truly wants for us) to subjugate our human decisions. God made all men with the right of free will. So, when we place our human desires over God's perfect will, then we reflect a love for the things of hell over against the things of God. In brief, it has to do with our love for sin which renders us hell bound.

3. **Unholy Leadership** can keep you from practicing what you preach–We are unholy–In Matthew **23**:**16-19** (NIV), Jesus said:

> "Woe to you, blind guides! ... You blind fools! ... You blind men!"[1]

---

1 A wise old unknown sage suggested that "Jesus presents the warnings to the Pharisees as He addresses hypocrisy in traditional worship; worship that had sight, but no substance."

4. Unhealthy Attitudes–In Matthew **23:23-24** (NIV), Jesus said:

> "Woe to you teachers of the law and Pharisees, you hypocrites! …you have neglected the more important matters of the law–justice, mercy and faithfulness…You blind guides! You strain out at gnat but swallow a camel."

5. Lures–We are hedonistic–In Matthew **23:25-26** (NIV), Jesus said,

> "Woe to you, teachers of the law and Pharisees, you hypocrites! You clean the outside of the cup and dish, but inside they are full of greed and self-indulgence. Blind Pharisee! First clean the inside of the cup and dish, and then the outside also will be clean."

6. Lies–We are holy rollers–In Matthew **23:27-28** (NIV), Jesus said,

> "Woe to you, teachers of the law and Pharisees, you hypocrites! You are like whitewashed tombs, which look beautiful on the outside but on the inside are full of dead men's bones and everything unclean. In the same way, on the outside you appear to people as righteous but on the inside you are full of hypocrisy and wickedness."

7. Lostness–We are heartless–In Matthew **23:29-33** (NIV), Jesus said,

> "Woe to you, teachers of the law and Pharisees, you hypocrites! …You snakes! You brood of vipers! How will you escape being condemned to hell?"

However, despite our life hindrances, despite our love hell-bound situation, despite our unwholesome leadership of un-holiness, despite our lust of un-healthiness, despite our lures of hedonism, despite our lies of being a holy roller, despite our lostness of heart, we have a Savior by the name of Jesus.

Who is able to give us life? Who is able to give us love? Who is able to give us leadership? Who is able to remove our lust? Who is able to remove our lures? Who is able to defeat our lies? Who is able to change our lostness?

Jesus Is The One!

1 "She will give birth to a Son, and you are to give Him the name Jesus, because He will save His people from their sins" (Matt. **1:21**, NIV)

2. "He died for us so that, whether we are awake or asleep, we may live together with Him" (1 Thess. **5:10**, NIV).

3. "In Him was life, and that life was the light of men. The light shines in the darkness, but the darkness has not understood it" (John **1:4-5**, NIV).

4. "If you remain in Me and My words remain in you, ask whatever you wish, and it will be given you" (John **15:7**, NIV).

Jesus is able to teach us how to practice what we preach! This is good news! Isaiah said,

> *But He was pierced for our transgressions,* [This Is Good News: Jesus Practiced What He Preached] *He was crushed for our iniquities;* [This Is Good News: Jesus Practiced What He Preached] *the punishment that brought us peace was upon Him,* [This Is Good News: Jesus Practiced What He Preached] *and by His wounds we are healed*
> ISAIAH **53:5**, NIV

Now We Can Practice What We Preach!

How is this possible for us to preach Jesus? *We need the mind of Christ.* Philippians **2:5** says, "Let this mind be in you which was also in Christ Jesus." We need the mind of Christ. But we will never get the mind of Christ, until we repent and come to Christ! Repent: *Metaneō*.[2] Change! It time for a change! Are You Ready to Practice What You Preach? If you are ready, say, "Yes! I'm ready!" And come and join the team!

Now Prove It!

It was at Calvary that Jesus practiced what He preached. He proved it to God. He proved it to Himself. He proved it to His mother, father, family, disciples, the Pharisees, Zealots, the lost, the left out, the poor, the blind, hungry, the pimps, the prostitutes, the Roman Government, the Jewish Sanhedrin Council, and ultimately to the entire world. Jesus preached that He would lay down His life and He did. He practiced what He preached.

We need to practice what we preach or don't waste man and God's time preaching something that we don't do or didn't even plan to do. Now come and put into practice what you have been preaching to others and put it into practice for yourself. And practice what you preach.

---

2 Richard Owen Roberts, *Repentance: The First Word of the Gospel* (Crossway Book, 2002), 24..

Chapter 14

Only God Can Make Things Grow

I planted the seed, Apollos watered it, but God made it grow. Do not deceive yourselves. If any one of you thinks he is wise by the standards of this age, he should become a "fool" so that he may become wise.
1 CORINTHIANS **3:6, 18**A, NIV

Paul wrote to the Corinthian church and reminded them, "I planted the seed, Apollos watered it, but God made it grow." Then, he said, "Do not deceive yourselves." Two words: *grow* and *deceive*. Growth and deception: deceptive growth. Why things won't grow: a growth deception! Only God can make things grow.

Man can't do a thing without God! Only God possesses the providential, supernatural, audacious power to cause un-cause-able things to come to fruition and abundant fruitfulness. John **15:7** says, "If you abide in Me, and My words abide in you, you will ask what you desire, and it shall be done for you." We may have much ability, knowledge, intellect, charisma, common sense, personality, smarts, style, looks, money, a nice big beautiful edifice and the rest, but if God does not show up and show out things just won't grow! In Genesis **1:3**, **1:6**, **1:9**, **1:11**, **1:14**, **1:20**, **1:24**, it says, "Let or Let there be...and it was."

Only God Can Make Things Grow

The Apostle Paul had received a word from the household (or *oikos*) of Chloe that there were factions that had developed in the church at Corinth. This was a genteel church. Lavished with vivacious gifts and talents galore, Paul called for unity, not disunity. His passion was for a cooperative, collaborative community of authentic Christian believers, eager to hurl the gospel of Jesus Christ from one end of the Greco-Roman Empire to the other. In the venue of this passion. Paul engages the Greco-Roman culture of his day to lift this divided Corinthian church out of murk and mire of sin and degradation.

This is a lengthy passage of Scripture. And as I have written in previous chapters, I want you to read God's Word. I don't know how to say it any other way than to say, read God's Word. Once again, some of you may not have read what I have written in the previous chapters. You may have picked this chapter to read because it simply captured you attention. If that is the case, then allow me to write what I've written a number of times in the previous chapters. Do not assume you know what my intent is. Read the entire chapter. Read all the passage of Scripture, even if you have read it hundreds of times. Read it one more time. I am utterly convinced that the Holy Spirit of God will still teach you new and wonderful things you would have never discovered if you had omitted reading it again. Paul said to the church at Corinth.

•Paul's Passionate Appeal

I appeal to you, brothers, in the name of our Lord Jesus Christ, that all of you agree with one another so that there may be no divisions among you and that you may be perfectly united in mind and thought. My brothers, some from Chloe's household have informed me that there are quarrels among you. What I mean is this: One of you says, "I follow Paul"; another, "I follow Apollos"; another, "I follow Cephas'"; still another, "I follow Christ."

• Paul's Penetrating Questions

Is Christ divided? Was Paul crucified for you? Were you baptized into the name of Paul? I am thankful that I did not baptize any of you except Crispus and Gaius, so no one can say that you were baptized into my name. (Yes, I also baptized the household of Stephanas; beyond that, I don't remember if I baptized anyone else.) For Christ did not send me to baptize, but to preach the gospel–not with words of human wisdom, lest the cross of Christ be emptied of its power.

• Paul's Powerful Message

For the message of the cross is foolishness to those who are perishing, but to us who are being saved it is the power of God. For it is written: "I will destroy the wisdom of the wise; the intelligence of the intelligent I will frustrate."

• **Paul's Passion in Pleasing God through the Person of Christ**

Where is the wise man? Where is the scholar? Where is the philosopher of this age? Has not God made foolish the wisdom of the world? For since in the wisdom of God the world through its wisdom did not know Him, God was pleased through the foolishness of what was preached to save those who believe. Jews demand miraculous signs and Greeks look for wisdom, but we preach Christ crucified: a stumbling block to Jews and foolishness to Gentiles, but to those whom God has called, both Jews and Greeks, Christ the power of God and the wisdom of God. For the foolishness of God is wiser than man's wisdom, and the weakness of God is stronger than man's strength.[1]

1 CORINTHIANS 1:10-25, NIV

Paul knew only God possesses the eternal wisdom to make things grow! Man's wisdom is no match for the wisdom of God. Man's power and influence are impotent. God and only God possess the power to make things grow. What complicated things was the issue of "infantile religion."[2] Andrew Murray identifies it in his work as Inner Life–inner growth of the inner man. Inner growth in Christ occurs when the believer accepts the fact that we are brothers and sisters in the Lord Jesus Christ. Paul wanted the church at Corinth to write this truth on the tablets of their hearts. However, Paul realized that they could not understand his message because they were fleshly. Read what Paul had to say about fleshly people. Paul says:

Brothers, I could not address you as spiritual but as worldly–mere infants in Christ. I gave you milk, not solid food, for you were not yet ready for it. Indeed, you are still not ready. You are still worldly. For since there is jealousy and quarreling among you, are you not world-ly? Are you not acting like mere men? For when one says, "I follow Paul," and another, "I follow Apollos," are you not mere men?" What, after all, is Apollos? And what is Paul? Only servants, through whom you came to believe as the Lord has assigned to each his task.[3]

1 CORINTHIANS 3:1-5 NIV

---

1 1 Cor. 1:10–ff., Insights: "Only God can make things grow." This denotes the sovereignty of God. Man's efforts are thwarted in the presence and face of God. When God appears, power and purpose is unveiled. First there is the power of God, and then there is the purpose of God, which is manifested through the divine presence of God. Richard Foster, *Prayer: Finding the Heart's True Home* (Harper Collins: New York, 1992), XI–XII.

2 Ibid., 1.

3 1 Cor. 3:1–ff., Insights: Paul calls for unity. Unity in Christ is a vivid picture of Christian maturity. The immature Christian is one who seeks his or her own way, thus he or she contaminates Christian unity and biblical harmony.

Did you read this powerful passage on being fleshly? What did the Holy Spirit of God say to you? Preaching for spiritual awakening will never happen in our modern culture unless we accept the fact that we need God to help us do His ministry. I have come to realize only God can make things grow. It is truly the work of the Spirit of God. God must make it happen. It is simply a matter of understanding the difference between milk people and meat people.

There will always be meat people and milk people. Milk people are outer life people, meat people are inner life people. Providentially, milk people can become meat people. How?

The answer is God! Man can't do a thing! From verses **1** to verse **6**, Paul uses the first person singular personal pronoun "I" and second person plural personal pronoun "you." He says, "I" and "you." "Us" or "we!" We can't do a thing without God.

Paul said in **1** Corinthians **3**:

"Brothers, I could not address you as spiritual..." Verse **2**a, Paul said, "I gave you milk, not solid food..." Verse **2**b, Paul said, "...for you were not yet ready for it." Verse **3**a, Paul said, "You are still worldly...jealousy and quarreling among you, are you not worldly?" Verse **3**b, Paul said, "Are you acting like mere men?" Verse **4**a, Paul said, "For when one says, 'I follow Paul,' and another, 'I follow Apollos'." Verse **4**b, Paul said, "'... are you not mere men?'" Finally, in verse **6**a, Paul said, "I planted the seed, Apollos watered it..."

Then from verse **6**b to the close of verse **23**, Paul turns to God! In **1** Corinthians **3:6**b, Paul says. "...but God made it grow." In verse **7**b, Paul said, "...but only God, who makes things grow." In verse **9**a, Paul said, "For we are God's fellow workers..." In verse **9**b, Paul said, "...you are God's field..." In verse **9**c, Paul said, "...you are God's building." Then in verse **10**, Paul says, "By the grace of God." In verse **11**b, Paul says, "...which is Jesus Christ." In verse **16**, Paul says, "Don't you know that you yourselves are God's temple and God's Spirit lives in you?" In verse **20**, Paul says, "The Lord knows." Then finally in verse **23**, Paul says, "...and you are of Christ, and Christ is of God." "Only God Can Make It Grow!" God is our ultimate solution for a successful ministry, nothing else will do. "Only God Can Make Things Grow!"

When God makes things grow–they grow. First, things will multiply. You will not be able to do the math. They will literally take off. That's what happened in Acts **2**; things just took off. They ran out of space in the existing church building. They had to expand and expand and expand. When God makes things grow, they will multiply.

Second, when God makes things grow, they will magnify the sufficiency of the Lord God Almighty. God would become bigger in the eyes of all people–both sinner and Saint. The bigger God gets, the greater the spirit of evangelism and church growth. Things will just happen. Growth occurs in ways no one can explain through the human intellect. All people will be able to say is this: "What a mighty God we serve."

Third, when God makes things grow, it will mystify the minds of men as we do the work of the Master. God's will be done, on earth as it is in heaven. Kingdom growth literally perplexes the minds of men. They will not understand how God does what He does with simple, ordinary people. They will ask questions. Such questions will cause them to realize their need for change. They will come to know you can't do a thing without God.

When man makes things grow, you do not get Kingdom growth. Why? The reasons are right before our eyes. Man can only attempt to manipulate the work of the Kingdom of God. God will not allow anyone to manipulate His work. You will have to answer to God Himself. So, don't attempt to manipulate God.

When man makes things grow, there will be huge mess ups. We are all mess-ups in the process of messing up. God is not the God of disorder, but the God of order. He is not the God of chaos; He is the God of cosmos. God is able to take chaos and transform it into cosmos. God can do anything but fail. Isn't that good news? The good news of the gospel is that Jesus is alive and well.

When man makes things grow, the glory does not go to God. Kingdom growth brings the real blessing and benefits as well as gives glory to Almighty God alone. Only God can make things grow!

While we realize more than ever that only God can make things grow, we have a problem–man is a sinner. In Romans 3:23, the Bible says, "For all have sinned and fall short of the glory of God." In Romans 6:23, "For the wages of sin is death, but the gift of God is eternal life in Christ Jesus our Lord."

How can sinful man work with a holy God? The answer is found in 1 Peter 1:16, "For it is written: "Be holy, because I am holy." The time has come to fall at the feet of Jesus and live. Come to His cross and live. Come right now! We've got to see Jesus. I saw Him for myself! He is my Lord! My life! My Love! My Hope! My Help! My Healer! My Provider! My Strength! My Savior! My all in all! He died! To set me free! He died! To save my soul! He died! But, He's coming back! Are you ready? Don't get ready! Be ready!

Chapter 15

Preach the Word: The Mouthpiece of God

Preach the Word; be prepared in season and out of season; correct,
rebuke and encourage–with great patience and careful instruction.
2 TIMOTHY **4:2**, NIV

God is not impressed with our opinions. He is equally not turned on by, or moved to tears with, what you and I think. As a matter of fact, the LORD God Almighty clearly says to each of us: "For My thoughts are not your thoughts, Nor are your ways My ways," (Isa. **55:8**). "For as the heavens are higher than the earth, so are My ways higher than your ways, and My thoughts than your thoughts" (Isa. **55:9**). The Bible goes on to say that, "There is a way that seems right to a man, but its end is the way of death" (Prov. **14:12**). That is why the Psalmist cries out, "Teach me Your way, O LORD, and I will walk in Your truth; give me an undivided heart, that I may fear your name" (Psa. **86:11**) forever, and ever, and ever.

Turning the Page

Consider what we are going to do with our dusty Bibles. I am talking about the Bibles that you have had for several years, but have not read. How much longer are you going to allow an unread Bible to continue to lie around your house? What are you going to do about that Bible in the back seat of your SUV? Will you continue to allow your family Bible to collect dust on the table in your beautiful family room? Why should anyone have a Bible that they have not read from cover to cover? It is literally a waste of cowhide and fallen oak trees to own an unused, unread Holy Bible.

Did you not know that the Word of God can literally change your life? It can change your attitude and your heart. It can change your conversation. It can change your family. It can change your children. It can change your marriage. It can change your mate. It can even change your giving to the church.

But a church that does not ascribe to the Word of God is a dead church. It is a church without power! It is a church without peace! It is a church without promise! It is a church without proper position in the Kingdom of God. Thus, it is a racist church. It is a black church, a red church, a green church, or a yellow church; but it is not God's Church. God's Holy Spirit will not and cannot dwell in an unclean, unholy temple like this!

The Ebony and Ivory Keys

What kind of church is your church today? Do the members of your church operate on, in, and through the Supernatural Power of God's Holy Righteous Word? When will you make it known throughout your region? A community, state, and nation needs to see, *"The Ebony and Ivory Keys on God's Divine Baby Grand Piano Playing together in Biblical Harmony and Melodious Grace,"* a community of people that is neither north nor south; that is hot for God, not cold or lukewarm. We should be a community of people that is, as Leith Anderson so eloquently puts it, *Dying for Change.* What would happen if our churches fail to use the Power of the WORD of God? What if we listened to the world more than to the WORD? What kind of influence do you think we would have in our city, state, nation, and the world? But on the other hand, suppose we decided to listen to the WORD more than to the world? What do you think would happen in our community here and beyond?

The Mouthpiece of God

But there is yet another question we must ask. Who did God assign as His *Mouthpiece* to preach His Word to us? Who is it that speaks for God today as His unique *Mouthpiece*? The Apostle Paul encouraged young Timothy to be the *Mouthpiece* of God. What a great honor to be the *Mouthpiece* of God.

It is a very awesome and fearful thing to be the *Mouthpiece* of God. There are times when I do not want to be His *Mouthpiece*, but just like Jeremiah, *"It's just like fire all shut up in my bones."* As a *Mouthpiece* of God, Isaiah cried, *"Woe to me! I am ruined..."* Then he said, *"Here am I. Send me!"* I'll go.

You will not win the popular vote being a *Mouthpiece* of God–but, it's the best job in town. I am literally amazed that God could use someone like me, being that I am from a small sawmill town in the southern state of Mississippi!

Paul tells Timothy about five basic things that he needs to remember as he preaches the WORD of God.

First: Know Who Your Audience Is—God

In the presence of God and of Christ Jesus, who will judge the living and the dead, and in view of His appearing and His kingdom, I give you this charge.

2 TIMOTHY **4:1**, NIV

This is critical. Our audience is God. God is the One who commands and demands our complete and undivided attention. He is a jealous God. He wants all of our attention—not just part of our attention. Our audience is God. Knowing this helps elevate our Christian performance on the stage of life for the glory of God.

Many years ago there was a man who was considered the greatest baritone on stage in the history of Broadway. His voice was smooth, crisp, colorful, and uniquely tasteful, inviting, and mesmerizing. When he would sing on Broadway, hoardes of people would begin lining up for days just to get a ticket to hear him. There were many who would literally camp out in the parking lot and the sidewalks to maintain their position in line to hear him sing.

Someone asked him, "What's your secret of success? How do you maintain your focus with literally thousands of people pressing through the doors to hear you sing? What is your secret?" Without pausing to take a breath, the renowned professional singer smiled and said confidently, "I know who my audience is." He went on to say, "Do you see that lady up there in the balcony? That's my wife. I never take my eyes off of her. I never look down at the people. I always look up and keep my eyes on my helpmeet."

In the same way, as Christians, we are to keep our heads up and look to the hills from where our help comes. Our help comes from the LORD, the maker of heaven and earth. He will not let our foot slip. He that keeps Israel neither slumbers nor sleeps. As Christians our audience is God—the God of Abraham, Isaac, and Jacob—the God of Moses, Joshua, and Ruth—the God of Matthew, Mark, Luke, and John. Our audience is God. "Let us fix our eyes on Jesus, the author and perfecter of our faith, who for the joy set before Him endured the cross, scorning its shame, and sat down at the right hand of the throne of God" (Heb. **12:2**, NIV). If we are going to be successful in whatever we do, we must know our audience. Beloved, our audience is God.

Is your focus on the LORD or are you looking at the stock market? Do you spend your time in daily prayer or do you spend your time "Day Trading?" Is God your audience or are the temporal things of this world your audience?

Second: Know What Your Season Is–Timing

Preach the Word; be prepared in season and out of season; correct, rebuke and encourage–with great patience and careful instruction. For the time will come when men will not put up with sound doctrine. Instead, to suit their own desires, they will gather around them a great number of teachers to say what their itching ears want to hear. They will turn their ears away from the truth and turn aside to myths. But you, keep your head in all situations, endure hardship, do the work of an evangelist, discharge all the duties of your ministry.

2 Timothy 4:2-5, NIV

Paul instructs young Timothy in understanding the value of timing. Divine timing takes into account the significance of knowing how to live an orderly life. Divine timing is connected to divine order, that is remembering that one comes before two, three follows two and so forth and so on. Timothy needed Paul's coaching. Paul's coaching arrived in the form of a pastoral epistle to Timothy.

Paul said to his young protégé, Timothy, "…be prepared in season and out of season." What does this mean? It means we must be ready for whatever comes our way. We should never drop our guard. Be ready to preach in the winter, when things are hard and the ground is frozen like granite. Be ready to preach in the spring, when God is renewing us, and is giving us more strength, more people, more joy, more love, hope, and help. Be ready to preach in the summer, when life is wonderful, the kids are happy, the wife is happy, and the job is great. Be ready to preach in the fall, when there is much color, yet there is a slight chill in the air and things are beginning to die. And finally, we've got to be ready to preach when the winter comes once again. We must prepare for all seasons.

Several years ago, I was at a hospital visiting one of the church members. I had been at the hospital for about an hour when a news flash occurred. The news report said, "A plane has just crashed into one of the buildings at the Trade Center in New York." Everyone at the hospital froze. Then a number of people bent to their knees in prayer. While we prayed, another plane crashed into the second skyscraper. As a nation, we were not ready for this.

Paul said to young Timothy, "Preach the Word…be prepared." If we are going to avert the dangers of this world, we must be prepared. We must be prepared in season, when things are going great. We must be prepared out of season, when things are horrible.

Preach the Word...*be prepared in season and out of season.*

Are you prepared? Are you prepared for the Second Coming of Jesus Christ? He's coming back! He's coming sooner than you or I think! Are you ready? Are you prepared? If you are not ready, then when will you get ready?

Third: Know Who Your Enemy Is–Satan

But mark this: There will be terrible times in the last days...People... having a form of godliness but denying its power.
2 TIMOTHY 3:1, 2, 5

Paul is writing about the power of darkness–Satan–the Devil himself. The people are not our enemies. Our enemy is Satan, Lucifer, the Devil, the malevolent one, the Prince of Darkness, or Baal. As a matter of fact, he is the enemy of God and everything good, wholesome, and righteous. Satan is always up to something evil and ungodly.

I once heard about a man who was so angry with the government and taxes, he decided he would get even. He came up with a plan. He purchased several drums of kerosene, doused his home, lit a match, and burned his one million dollar home to the ground. He said, to himself, "I'll show Uncle Sam. He'll never over tax me again." Then it struck him. He had just burned his house down and he still owed the bank!

Far too often, our anger punishes the wrong person. We need to know who our real enemy is. Our real enemy is not Uncle Sam. Our real enemy is Satan. Paul says to young Timothy:

But mark this: There will be terrible times in the last days. People will be lovers of themselves, lovers of money, boastful, proud, abusive, disobedient to their parents, ungrateful, unholy, without love, unforgiving, slanderous, without self-control, brutal, not lovers of the good, treacherous, rash, conceited, lovers of pleasure rather than lovers of God–having a form of godliness but denying its power. Have nothing to do with them.
2 TIMOTHY 3:1-5, NIV

Furthermore, Paul adds,

They are the kind who worm their way into homes and gain control over weak-willed women, who are loaded down with sins and are swayed by all kinds of evil desires, always learning but never able to

acknowledge the truth. Just as Jannes and Jambres opposed Moses, so also these men oppose the truth–men of depraved minds, who, as far as the faith is concerned, are rejected. But they will not get very far because, as in the case of those men, their folly will be clear to everyone.
2 TIMOTHY **3:6-9**, NIV

Are you fighting the right enemy? Are you angry at the right person? Do you know how to fight this evil spirit? You don't fight fire with fire. You fight fire with faith. Faith in Almighty God–Let God fight for you…He knows how to handle Satan. Satan's days are numbered. Don't worry. God is in control. Just trust Him.

Fourth: Know Where Your Power Is–The Bible

You, however, know all about my teaching, my way of life, my purpose, faith, patience, love, endurance… and how from infancy you have known the holy Scriptures.
2 TIMOTHY **3:10, 15**, NIV

Our power is in the Bible. From Genesis to Revelation, from Psalm to Proverbs, Matthew, Mark, Luke and John, Isaiah, Jeremiah, Lamentation, Ezekiel, Daniel, Hosea, Genesis, Exodus, Leviticus, Numbers, Deuteronomy, Joshua, Judges, and Ruth. Our power is in the Bible–God's Word.

When I was young in the faith, I used to think my power was in my ability to make people happy. I thought being nice and living the Christian life would help me make many friends. I have come to realize that I have no power to make anyone happy. My power is in God's Word–The Bible. *The B.I.B.L.E., yes, that's the book for me, I stand alone on the Word of God, the B.I.B.L.E.–* The Bible. Paul instructs young Timothy with these words:

All Scripture is God-breathed and is useful for teaching, rebuking, correcting and training in righteousness, so that the man of God may be thoroughly equipped for every good work.
2 TIMOTHY **3:16-17**, NIV

Like Timothy, *"Do you know your Audience?* Like Timothy, *"Do you know your Season?* Like Timothy, *"Do you know your Enemy?* And, like Timothy, *"Do you know who your Power Source Is? Your Power Source is God!*
But there is one more thing you need to know.

Fifth: Know Who Your Savior Is—Jesus Christ

Is Jesus Christ your Savior and your Lord? Jesus is eternal, John 1:1. Jesus is omnipresent, Matthew 28:20. Jesus is omniscient, John 16:30. Jesus is omnipotent, John 5:19. Jesus is immutable, Hebrews 1:12. Jesus is the Creator, John 1:3. Jesus forgives sin, Matthew 9:2. Jesus was raised from the dead, John 5:25. Jesus is the Great I AM, John 8:58. Jesus is Immanuel, Matthew 1:22. Jesus is the Son of Man, Matthew 9:6. Jesus is the Son of God, John 10:36. Jesus is Lord, Matthew 7:21. Jesus is God, John 1:1. Don't wait too late to make sure you know Jesus as your Savior.

One day, a daughter went to visit her dad in the hospital. He had never been sick. He went in for a routine stress test. When she arrived, a host of medical doctors met both she and her husband and said. "We don't know what happened but…" He died. She was too late. Don't wait too late! Whatever you are going to do, do it now!

> *For I am already being poured out like a drink offering, and the time has come for my departure. I have fought the good fight, I have finished the race, I have kept the faith. Now there is in store for me the crown of righteousness, which the Lord, the righteous Judge, will award to me on that day–and not only to me, but also to all who have longed for his appearing.*
>
> 2 TIMOTHY 4:6-8, NIV

Don't wait too late.

Will you wait until next Sunday? Will you wait too late? Too late! Too late! Too late! Don't wait too late? Or will you do it now? Don't wait too late? He was wounded for our transgressions. He was bruised for our iniquities and by His stripes we are healed! Don't wait too late! Too late! Too late! DON'T WAIT TOO LATE! What are you going to do?

In the book of Revelations, the Bible says, "Jesus is coming back." Will you give Him your life? Will you come to Him? Will you say, "Yes, Lord Jesus I'm ready!"

I said, "Yes! Yes, Lord Jesus, yes!" Are you ready to say, "Yes?" Now, it's your time to say, "Yes." Dr. Billy Graham said, "Your yes ought to be done publicly." Would you like to be a better teenager, father, husband and person today?

How do you know that the Word of God has been preached with power? It is when you say, "Yes!"

When you say, "Yes," six things will be evident in your life and you will willingly embrace six profound life-changing principles with readiness and great joy.

The Six Life-Changing Principles in a Word-Driven Life

1. You will embrace sound *teaching*
2. You will embrace strong *rebuking*
3. You will embrace straight *correcting*
4. You will embrace simple *training*
5. You will embrace significant *encouragement*
6. You will embrace supernatural *salvation*

Jesus died on the cross to set us free. He gave up everything in order for us to have abundant life.

Surely He has borne our griefs and carried our sorrows; yet we esteemed Him stricken, smitten by God, and afflicted. But He was wounded for our transgressions, He was bruised for our iniquities; the chastisement for our peace was upon Him, and by His stripes we are healed.

ISAIAH **53:4-5**

…Confess…and…Come… Don't wait too late!

Chapter 16

Is Our Nation In Trouble?

If my people, who are called by my name, will humble themselves and pray and seek my face and turn from their wicked ways, then will I hear from heaven and will forgive their sin and will heal their land.
2 CHRONICLES 7:14, NIV

In his book, *Enough is Enough: A Call to Christian Involvement,* Dr. Rick Scarborough writes:

> The founding fathers started a number of colleges and universities between 1636 and 1769, and all but one was distinctly Christian. In 1636, *Harvard* was established by the Puritans. In 1693, *William and Mary* was established by the Anglicans. In 1701, *Yale* was established by the Congregationalists. In 1746, *Princeton* was established by the Presbyterians. In 1754, *King's College* was established by the Anglicans. In 1764, *Brown* was established by the Baptists. In 1766, *Rutgers* was established by the Dutch Reformed Believers. And finally, in 1769, *Dartmouth* was established by the Congregationalists.[1]

Today, many are shocked to discover that most of the nation's Ivy League schools were established by Christians, and these schools of higher learning held fast to the Scriptures as the foundation and authority of all truth. How much have we changed since those days? From establishing institutions of higher learning, to being ignored as any influence in education, we have changed for the worse. In our day, Christians who are speaking out about their deep convictions and faith in the Lord Jesus Christ are often branded as religious extremists.[2]

---

1 Rick Scarborough, "American Institutions were Built on Biblical Truth," in *Enough is Enough: A Call to Christian Involvement* (Springfield: 21st Century Press Publishing Company, 2004), 55.
2 Ibid., 55.

Is Our Nation In Trouble?

Are we in trouble politically, socially, economically, morally, and most of all, are we in trouble with God?

Have we elevated the power of the office of President, over the power of the office of the Prince of Peace? Have we sought the sufficiency of the good of men over the supremacy of the grace of God? Have we relied on man's solutions, as opposed to the Master's sovereignty? Do we have "In God We Trust" on the face of our money, but "In Government We Trust" as the foundation of our faith? Do we appear religious and righteous on the outside, but on the inside are filled with dead men's bones? Have we chosen to be politically correct but truthfully, are we morally and spiritually bankrupt and are we desperately in need of a mighty moving of the Holy Spirit of God? Is our nation in trouble? Are we in trouble with God?

In America, we appear to care more about the creation and the creature than we do about the Creator and the Christ. In America, we appear to care more about our baseball than we do about our Bibles. In America, we appear to care more about our football than we do about our fellowship in the congregations of the believers. In America, we appear to care more about ourselves than we do about our Savior. In America, we appear to care more about our work than we do about our worship. In America, we appear to care more about winning a soccer match than we do about winning a soul for the Maker. In America, we appear to care more about Hollywood than we do about our Heavenly Father's House. In America, we appear to care more about our cars, our clothes, our homes, our toys, our vacations, our money, our games, and electronic gadgets and technology than we do about our God. In America, we appear to care more about getting and giving Christmas gifts than we do about glorifying God and giving ourselves for the cause of Christ.

Is Our Nation In Trouble?

Are we in trouble politically, socially, economically, morally, and most of all, are we in trouble with God?

Why do you think that we are in trouble with God? According to the Scriptures, we are in trouble with God because we have refused *"to turn from our wicked ways."* 2 Chronicles 7:14 (NIV) says, "…If my people, who are called by My name, will humble themselves and pray and seek My face and turn from their wicked ways..." Our nation has *some wicked ways.*

The setting of **2** Chronicles **7** reveals that the temple of God had been completed. God then had a prominent place at the center of Israel's worship. Solomon did what David could not do. He completed the building of the temple of God in Jerusalem. Everything appeared to be going great. The Bible declared in **2** Chronicles **7:1** (NIV), "When Solomon finished praying, fire came down from heaven and consumed the burnt offering and the sacrifices, and the glory of the LORD filled the temple. "

God was blessing Israel, just like God has been blessing our nation. Israel was so blessed that the priest could not even enter the temple of the Lord because the glory of the Lord filled the temple. In the same way, God has blessed America so much so until our pulpits no longer preach on our sinful ways, our evil hearts, our wicked spirits, our unrighteous lifestyles, our disrespectful behaviors, our unwholesome divisions, hell fire, eternal death, judgment, punishment, and the like.

The Bible said that the Lord filled the temple with His presence. God was everywhere. Many people were on their faces before God. Others were worshiping the Lord and saying, *"He is good; His love endures forever."* Then Solomon offered sacrifices to the Lord. He sacrificed twenty-two thousand head of cattle and one hundred and twenty thousand sheep and goats. The Levites played musical instruments. They were praising God as they had seen King David do in times past, saying, *"His love endures forever."* Then the priests blew their trumpets, and all Israel stood on their feet and many more offerings were given to the Lord.

When Solomon had finished the temple of the Lord and his royal palace, the Lord said to Solomon, *"I have heard your prayers and have chosen this place for Myself as a temple for sacrifices."* All was going well. Everybody was happy. Just like in America when many of us got our "stimulus checks." The banks were happy. GM and Chrysler was happy. Wall Street was thrilled and everybody in our nation was so happy because the "stimulus money" was flowing like milk and honey. But, our nation is still in trouble.

Yet, we appear to being doing well. Our churches are getting bigger. Many churches have more people in worship today. Some churches have two, three, four, and even five worship services a week. A number of churches are open 24/7 [that is 24 hours a day, 7 days a week–with full recreational centers, family life centers, indoor jungle gyms, swimming pools, softball fields, camps, retreat centers, cafes, Starbucks, clinics, counseling centers, numerous ministries, radio and TV programs, libraries, bookstores, missions programs, and the rest. Yet, our nation is in trouble. Our nation is in trouble with God, [why] because we have *some wicked ways.*

What made matters worse was that Israel, like America, appeared to be doing extremely well, yet they were still in trouble with God and did not even know there was a problem. Our nation is no different than Israel. We as a nation appear to be doing well. The stock market is back up. Home sales are increasing. Christmas shopping was up. But we are still in trouble with God. The Lord said to Israel:

> *When I shut up the heavens so that there is no rain, or command locusts to devour the land or send a plague among my people, if my people, who are called by my name, will humble themselves and pray and seek my face and turn from their wicked ways, then will I hear from heaven and will forgive their sin and will heal their land.*
> 2 CHRONICLES 7:13-14, NIV

Israel was in trouble with God and right now our nation is in trouble with God, too. But what do we need to do to avert this trouble with God? What is the solution that will bring resolution to this situation?

Solution 1

First, we need to *act* like we belong to God. God purchased us by His blood at Calvary. He died for us. We are supposed to *act* like we are His people. We are supposed to *act* like His children. We are supposed to *act* like the elect, the called out, and the redeemed children of God. Further, we are supposed to *act* like we are the light of the world, the salt of the earth, and the seed of Abraham. We need to *act* like we belong to God.

Several years ago, a man in a local small town opened up a medical doctor's office in his name. He hired staff. In a matter of years, he had treated thousands of people. He served on countless boards, agencies, and commissions, until one day, someone from another town informed them that he was not a doctor, but a charlatan. He was a fake. He was bogus. He was not an MD. He fooled hundreds if not thousands of people, because he acted like he was a physician; but he did not fool the authorities. You can fool many people about being a Christian; but you can't fool God. We need to *act* like we belong to God.

God said, "*I am your God and you are My people.*" We ought to **act** like we belong to Him. God created us. He made us in His image and likeness (Gen. **2**). He blew the breath of life into us and we became a living soul. That is a *nephesh hayah.* He made us both *adam* and *adamah* [man and woman]. He made us both *'esh* and *'eshah* [male and female]. He did all this for us in the beginning, as revealed in Genesis Chapters **1** and **2**. We are God's people. We belong to God and we need to **act** like we belong to Him.

In **2** Corinthians **5:17**, the Scripture states, "Therefore, if anyone is in Christ, he is a new creation; old things have passed away; behold, all things have become new." Do you **act** like you belong to God? Are you a new creation? Are you changed? Do you **act** like you belong to God? Are you redeemed by the blood of Jesus? If not, then what will it take for you to **act** like you belong to God?

Solution 2

Second, we need to **look** like we belong to God. We ought to **look** differently. We ought to **look** different than the world. Often, it is difficult in America, to tell a Christian from a lost person. Too often, in America, we **look** just like the world. We talk like the world, live like the world, act like the world. We need to **look** like we belong to God.

When my wife and I were in seminary in New Orleans, we decided to go to Mardi Gras. Our son, Beau [age 3] said, "Daddy that man looks like a woman. Is he a she?" I said, "I'm not sure, son. He or she is wearing a mask and we will never know, until he or she removes his or her mask." We need to look like we belong to God.

Unfortunately, Christians in America too often hide behind the mask of pride. The Bible says, "*Pride goeth before the fall.*" The Bible says, "*God will humble the proud.*" God said to Israel, just as He is saying to America, "*If My people, who are called by My name, will humble themselves...*" Being humble is more than words. Humility is action, not anticipation. Humility is what we do and not what we say. Humility has to do with character. Character is what we **look** like to a sinful and dying world. Humility is a matter of choice that comes out of character. We choose to be humble. Sincere prayer never comes before Christian humility. Prayer and humility operate hand-in-glove. Prayer is the glove and humility is the hand of character in the glove. In America, we are God's people and we need to **look** like we belong to God.

In James 4:10, "Humble yourselves in the sight of the Lord, and He will lift you up." As God's people, we are to be humble before the Lord and the Lord will lift us up. Jesus said in John 12:32, "And I, if I am lifted up from the earth, will draw all peoples to Myself." We are to *look* like we belong to God.

Do you *look* like you belong to God? If not, then ask God to give you a spiritual makeover. In America, we need to *look* like we belong to Him. So, what are you going to do? Will you choose to humble yourself in the glove of prayer and *look* like you belong to Almighty God?

Solution 3

Third, we need to *live* like we belong to God. As Christians in America, our lives ought to be different than the world. The way we *live* should be a picture of Christ. We cannot *live* like the devil through the week and then pretend to be Christians on Wednesday night, Sunday morning, and Sunday night. We need to *live* like we belong to God.

Once there was a Christian business man who was very active in his church, but he did not *live* like it. He was a good Bible teacher, but he did not *live* like it. He was at church every Sunday, Wednesday, and Saturday, but he didn't *live* like it. One day, while on an out-of-town business trip, he decided to take his clients to "the boat" to gamble. He thought this would help to obtain their business. Because he lived like his clients, he started gambling. At the end of the day, he had won so much money, he decided to donate a large sum of it to the church's building fund. But the pastor refused to take the money. The business man was shocked. He then asked a number of people, "Why won't he take my money?" Immediately, a little old lady responded to his question with these words. "You don't live like you know God, sonny."

Far too many Christians in America *live* like we do not belong to the Lord. We are unforgiving, unloving, ungrateful, unkind, and uncommitted to the things of God. Far too many Christians in America have some wicked ways. Wicked ways suggest how we *live* out our Christianity on a daily basis in our homes, communities, and in our churches. Wicked ways denote our walk. Our walk addresses our life-choices or lifestyle. Our walk should always match our talk. If not, then our walk can cause others to stumble over our unfaithful feet. If we are God's people, then we need to *live* like we belong to Him. We are no longer under personal ownership; but we are under divine ownership. Divine ownership means "new management." Our property, that is our soul, has a new manager, and that new manager is God–the Counselor–The Holy Spirit, who teaches us how to live under truth-management. We are no longer the boss. We are no longer in control of what we want to do or say.

Either God is in control of us or Satan is in control us. We cannot have two bosses. We cannot serve two masters. It is either Satan or God, our way or His Way. We cannot have it both ways. Therefore, it is either His Word and His Way or our word and our way. In America, we need to *live* like we belong to God.

> *And those who are Christ's have crucified the flesh with its passions and desires. If we live in the Spirit, let us also walk in the Spirit. Let us not become conceited, provoking one another, envying one another.*
> GALATIANS **5:24-26**

Do you *live* like you belong to God? If you don't, then what are you going to do? Will you choose to *live* like you belong to the Lord or *live* like you belong to Lucifer? Believe me, people do know the difference. Most importantly, God knows too.

Good News, If...

If we *act* like, *look* like, and *live* like we belong to God, then God said in **2** Chronicles **7:14**b (NIV), *"...then will I hear from heaven and will forgive their sin and will heal their land."* Notice what God says, if we *act* like, *look* like, and *live* like we belong to Him. God says, first, *"I will allow you to hear from Me [heaven]."* Second, God says, *"I will forgive your sin."* That is to say, "God will totally forgive us of all sin." Listen, the root of sin is pride. Then, third, God says, *"I will heal your land."* Look, the land has to do with our souls. God says, *"I will heal your soul."*

But if we do not *act* like, *look* like, and *live* like we belong to Him, then God said,

> *But if you turn away and forsake the decrees and commands I have given you and go off to serve other gods and worship them, then I will uproot Israel from my land, which I have given them, and will reject this temple I have consecrated for my Name. I will make it a byword and an object of ridicule among all peoples.*
> **2** CHRONICLES **7:19**, NIV

God will reject them and make them a byword if they do not *act* like, *look* like, and *live* like we belong to Him. Then, "People will answer, 'Because they have forsaken the LORD, the God of their fathers, who brought them out of

Egypt, and have embraced other gods, worshiping and serving them—that is why He brought all this disaster on them'" (**2 Chron. 7:22**, NIV).

Are you in trouble? Physically, psychologically, economically, relationally, emotionally, mentally, morally, and spiritually; but most of all are you in trouble with God?

Does God have a case against you? Are you in trouble with God? If you are in trouble with God, then there is a solution–Calvary! Isaiah **53:5** says. "But He was wounded for our transgressions, He was bruised for our iniquities; the chastisement for our peace was upon Him, and by His stripes we are healed."

Broken Commandments

I believe our nation is in trouble! As a nation we have broken Commandment #**1**: We are serving other gods; Commandment #**2**: We have made many idols; Commandment #**3**: We curse God's Name; Commandment #**4**: We are not honoring the Sabbath Day; Commandment # **5**: We are not honoring our fathers and mothers; Commandment #**6**: We murder; Commandment #**7**: We commit adultery; Commandment # **8**: We steal; Commandment #**9**: We lie; and Commandment #**10**: We covet. Our nation and our churches are in trouble! Maybe you are in trouble, too! Life troubles, marital troubles, family troubles, children troubles, economic troubles, or spiritual troubles? Troubles! Trouble! Trouble! Trouble…!

Get Out of Trouble

So, how do we get out of trouble?

- Romans **10:9** say, "that if you confess with your mouth the Lord Jesus and believe in your heart that God has raised Him from the dead, you will be saved."
- Romans **6:23** says, "For the wages of sin is death, but the gift of God is eternal life in Christ Jesus our Lord."
- Romans **3:23** says, "for all have sinned and fall short of the glory of God."
- **1** John **1:9** says, "If we confess our sins, He is faithful and just to forgive us our sins and to cleanse us from all unrighteousness."
- Jesus said, in Matthew **4:17**, "Repent, for the kingdom of heaven is at hand."
- Peter said, in Acts **2:38**, "Repent, and let every one of you be baptized in the name of Jesus Christ for the remission of sins; and you shall receive the gift of the Holy Spirit."

Jesus died to take away our troubles. *He died* to set us free. *He died* until the sun refused to shine. *He died* until the moon dripped in blood. *He died* until the stars fell from the sky. *He died* until dead bodies got up from the grave. *He died* until the Centurion said, "Surely He must have been the Son of God." *He died* so that we might have a right to the tree of life. Jesus died! But early that Resurrection Sunday morning, He got up with all power in His hands.

Power to save souls from hell! *Power* to take the sting out of death, hell, and the grave! Now we've got the *power*, too. We are no longer in trouble. Listen,

> God Bless America, Land that I love. Stand beside her, and guide her thru the night with a light from above. From the mountains, to the prairies, To the oceans, white with foam, God bless America, My home sweet home. God bless America, my home sweet home.[3]

If you love our nation, get on your knees and pray for our nation. Pray before it's too late! Jesus loves us all and He wants us to *act like, look like,* and *live like* we belong to God.

---

3 Irving Berlin, "God Bless America," words and music created and written by Irving Berlin, and © Copyright 1938.

Chapter 17

Behold I Set Before You An Open Door

"I know your deeds. See, I have placed before you an open door that no one can shut. I know that you have little strength, yet you have kept my word and have not denied my name."

REVELATION 3:8

Jesus is always concerned about His church. He is never without words of warning, witness, and wisdom for His people. We need to listen to Jesus and not to the voices of our culture. The voices of the culture are deadly and dangerous. No man or woman can survive eating from the garden of human wisdom and understanding. Christ calls us to a higher order of life. This higher order of life is one available to those who are willing to seek the Lord where He is found and call upon Him while He is yet near. Listen now to the words of Jesus from the book of the Revelation. Jesus said.

• God Already Know

To the angel of the church in Philadelphia write: These are the words of him who is holy and true, who holds the key of David. What he opens no one can shut, and what he shuts no one can open. I know your deeds. See, I have placed before you an open door that no one can shut. I know that you have little strength, yet you have kept my word and have not denied my name. I will make those who are of the synagogue of Satan, who claim to be Jews though they are not, but are liars–I will make them come and fall down at your feet and acknowledge that I have loved you. Since you have kept my command to endure patiently, I will also keep you from the hour of trial that is going to come upon the whole world to test those who live on the earth. I am coming soon. Hold on to what you have, so that no one will take your crown. Him who overcomes I will make a pillar in the temple of my God. Never again will he leave it. I will write on him the name of my

> *God and the name of the city of my God, the new Jerusalem, which is coming down out of heaven from my God; and I will also write on him my new name. He who has an ear, let him hear what the Spirit says to the churches.*
>
> REVELATION **3:7-13**, NIV

Listen closely to what the Spirit of the Living God has placed upon my heart. I want you to know that my message does not come from what I want to say. My message comes only from what my Heavenly Father has placed deeply upon my heart. Therefore, my subject comes from the heart and soul of Revelation **3:8** in the "a" section of the text. Jesus says, "*I know your deeds. See, I have placed before you an open door that no one can shut. I know that you have little strength, yet you have kept my word and have not denied my name.*" The King James Version of the Bible reports Revelation **3:8**b, in this manner, "*...behold, I have set before thee an open door.*"

Elevate in 2010

The Church of Philadelphia is the sixth of seven churches of Asia Minor. Jesus instructed John, while on the Isle of Patmos, to write concerning the end times. The word, Philadelphia is made up of the welding of two words, "*philos*" (i.e., love) and "*adelphos*" (i.e., brother or brotherly). The city of Philadelphia is the city of brotherly love. Thus, Jesus says, "...behold, I put before thee an open door." Not a cracked door, but an open door. I agree with the countless number of exegetical expositors that the open door is a profound door of opportunity.

I believe in the same way that God has placed before us an open door–a door of opportunity. It is a door of advancement. It is a door of growth. It is a door of success. It is a door of prosperity. It is a door where we the members of God's church will elevate in 2010. In other words, God has seen our faithfulness. God has witnessed our spirit of great determination. God has seen us as His people remaining focused on the power of God and the love of Jesus. And I believe God has said, "The time has come for us as God's people to elevate in 2010."

The Apostle Paul said, in Romans **8:28**, We are more than conquerors in the Lord Jesus Christ. We already have the victory! We are already blessed! We already have God's favor. We are ready to take back everything the devil has stolen from us. We are ready. That is why Jesus said in Revelation **3:8**, "*...behold, I put before thee an open door.*" But, why did Jesus put this open door before His church?

Heretical Teaching

According to Canon L. Morris, Principal of Ridley College, in his exegesis of Revelation 3, the church at Philadelphia had been very faithful.[1] Morris said that the church, "had not embraced heretical teaching."[2] Heretical teaching is the kind of teaching that does not exalt the name of Jesus. Heretical teaching is the kind of teaching that does not rest on the supernatural power of God. Heretical teaching is the kind of teaching that is void of supernatural revelation, spiritual inspiration, and divine illumination. Heretical teaching denies the doctrine of the Trinity. Heretical teaching rejects the virgin birth of Jesus Christ. Heretical teaching takes the position that Jesus is not the only way to the Father. Heretical teaching does not save sin-sick souls. Heretical teaching is Gnostic in nature. Heretical teaching chooses to dumb down the Good News. Heretical teaching does not bring conviction and spiritual transformation of the human heart. Heretical teaching is not of God.

Dr. Morris went on to say, "That the Christians in the city of Philadelphia experienced great persecution as a result of their firm stand on the faith against heretical teaching."[3] The church boldly and confidently believed God, and it refused to allow anyone or anything to stop them from doing otherwise. For these reasons, Jesus said, God had placed "before them an open door." The open door, according to Morris, was a door of missionary opportunity. It was a door to spread the gospel of Jesus Christ. It was a door to advance the name of Christ and to make Him fully known in the Regions of Mysia, Lydia, and Phrygia.[4] In an area that was called "the gateway city;" the gateway to the East.[5] Philadelphia, this Hellenistic or Greek City was a very prosperous city.[6] It was a city in a very strategic situation. It was a city that flourished in commerce as well as a city that was a center of the worship of many other gods. Philadelphia was a temple city. Philadelphia was a city with many hot springs. Yet, because of the faithfulness of the church members in the city of Philadelphia, Jesus said, "…behold, I put before thee an open door."

As God's people, let me say it again, we are standing at edge of that same door today. We are standing at the open door of advancement, the open door of

---

1 Canon Leon Morris, *The Revelation of St. John* (Grand Rapids: William B. Eerdmans Publishing Company, 1981), p. 77.
2 Ibid., p. 78.
3 Ibid.
4 Ibid., p. 77.
5 Ibid., p. 79.
6 Ibid.

blessings, the open door of promotion, the open door of elevation and exalta-
tion; the open door is a door of great success, just like the church at Philadelphia witnessed. And just like that church, it is time for us to do as they did and
that is to elevate in **2010**. But, why would God place before us an open door?
I believe the answer is clear.

Our Labor

First, The Lord Knows Our Labor (deeds)–v. **8**a. Our labor is about our
faithfulness to God. As God's people, we must be faithful to God. And God
is very proud of your faithfulness–just like the faithfulness of Hananiah
(Shadrach), Mishael (Meshach) and Azariah (Abednego). The Hebrew name
Hananiah means "Yahweh demonstrates amazing grace."[7] The Hebrew name
Mishael means, "Who indeed is what God is and always is."[8] And the Hebrew name Azariah means "Jehovah helps."[9] The Babylonian or slave name
Shadrach probably means, "Under, the command or commanded by the Su-
merian moon-god, Aku;"[10] the Babylonian or slave name Meshach probably
means "Who is what Aku is?"[11]; and the Babylonian or slave name Abednego
means "servant of Nego/Nebo[12] or Nabu."[13]

I'm so glad that the Lord knows our labor and not the Babylonian god Aku
or the god Nego or Nebo or Nabu or any other Babylonian god. I'm so glad
that the Lord knows our labor and our God is none other than Jehovah God;
the God of Abraham, Isaac, and Jacob. God knows our labor.

God has been with us from the very first step on our journey. As God's
people, God has not simply been with us; God has been within us, as well. That
is why in Revelation **3:8**a Jesus says, *"I know your deeds. See, I have placed
before you an open door that no one can shut."* So, the Lord knows our labor.

Our Life

Second–The Lord Knows Our Life–v. **8**b. Our life is more than just the
compilation of anthropomorphic DNA or bio-life. Our God knows our spiri-

---

7 Kenneth Baker, *The NIV Study Bible* (Grand Rapids: Zondervan Publishing House,
1995), p. 1291.

8 Ibid.

9 Ibid.

10 Ibid.

11 Ibid.

12 C. J. Ball, "Nebo, the Assyrian-Babylonian god," *Light from the East or the Witness of
the Moments*, 169, http://books.google.com/books?id=RTiTQSD_WusC&pg=PA169&dq=bab
ylonian+god+Nebo&sig= N2HJ_ Y2N2bBILpp5BFJeB52XagY.

13 Ibid.

tual life as Saints. God knows our life in Christ as His people. This is known as the Spirit-filled life of the believer. God knows that the Holy Ghost dwells in us. We are His people. At God's church, we have our BA Degree–our Born Again Degree. That is why Jesus said to Nicodemus in John **3**, that which is born of the flesh is flesh and that which is born of the spirit is spirit. This is called the new birth. The BA Degree!

Yet, we are still not perfect. But we are being perfected in Christ every day. We are not all that we need to be; but we are becoming more like Christ every day. That is way Jesus said, in Revelation **13:8**b, *"I know that you have little strength, yet you have kept My word and have not denied My name."*

Our Love

First, the Lord knows our labor. Second, the Lord knows our life. But, third and most important, the Lord Knows Our Love, v. **9**. Love is the most excellent way! There are many ways to do many things at the Lord's church, but there is no better way than the most excellent way–Love! At God's church, you just can't beat love. At God's church, you can't outdo love. At God's church, you can't constrict love. At God's church, you can't kill love. That is why at God's church, we shout out that love is the most excellent way! Love is in every vessel at God's church.

Paul said that this love is found in clay pots.

But we have this treasure in earthen vessels, that the excellence of the power may be of God and not of us. We are hard-pressed on every side, yet not crushed; we are perplexed, but not in despair; persecuted, but not forsaken; struck down, but not destroyed–always carrying about in the body the dying of the Lord Jesus, that the life of Jesus also may be manifested in our body.

2 CORINTHIANS **4:7-10**

In **1** John **3**, John said that this love is the door from death to life. The Lord knows our love, Saints. This is not simply affectionate love, Saints, but this is atoning love. From a theological perspective, atoning love is none other than sacrificial love–Christ being nailed to Calvary's Cross! This is true love, Saints! That is why in Revelation **3:9**, Jesus said, "I will make those who are of the synagogue of Satan, who claim to be Jews though they are not, but are liars–I will make them come and fall down at your feet and acknowledge that I have loved you.

Our Longsuffering

First, the Lord knows our labor. Second, the Lord knows our life. Third, the Lord knows our love. Fourth, and finally, the Lord Knows Our Longsuffering, v. **10**. The Lord has seen our longsuffering. God has been pleased with our level of commitment to Him. God has smiled on us. God has been watching us. And God wants us to know that He has heard our cry. And that He is on our side.

The Bible says,

Now to him who is able to do immeasurably more than all we ask or imagine, according to his power that is at work within us, to him be glory in the church and in Christ Jesus throughout all generations, for ever and ever! Amen.
EPHESIANS **3:20-21**, NIV

Isn't our God able, Saints? Has He not kept us, Saints? Has He not been faithful, Saints? Has He not carried us through, Saints? Has He not been with us all the way, Saints? Don't we serve a God that can do anything but fail, Saints? God is able to do what He said that He would do, Saints. And now He deserves all the glory, the honor and all the praise from each and every one of us, Saints! We must endure, Saints, despite our trials!

That is why Jesus said to the church at Philadelphia, in verse **10** (NIV), "Since you have kept My command to endure patiently, I will also keep you from the hour of trial that is going to come upon the whole world to test those who live on the earth." Jesus knows our Labor, our Life, our Love and our Longsuffering.

Furthermore, He made us three promises.

The Triune Promises of God

First, He promised to empower us. In verse **11** (NIV), Jesus says, "I am coming soon. Hold on to what you have, so that no one will take your crown." Second, He promised to establish us. In verse **12a** (NIV), Jesus says, "Him who overcomes I will make a pillar in the temple of my God. Never again will he leave it." Third, our God has promised to elevate us.

At Calvary, they elevated Him when they lifted up the cross. He got so high, until death was defeated, the grave was denied, and the glory of God came down. In verse **12b-13**, Jesus says, "I will write on him the name of my God and the name of the city of my God, the new Jerusalem, which is coming down out of heaven from my God; and I will also write on him my new name. He who has an ear, let him hear what the Spirit says to the churches."

Walking Through the Open Door

Behold, I set before you an open door. Come and walk through that door today. Come To Jesus! However, there may be some people reading, who are too stubborn to step out of disobedience and leap across the threshold of a changed life. Some people do not want to change. They would rather die and go to hell than to change and give their life to Jesus Christ.

Unfortunately for them, the door will close right in their face. This open door will not always remain open. One day the door is going to close. The door is open now, but soon it will be completely bolted closed. It is a door that no man can open and a door that no man can shut. It is open now but it will not remain open. If you are lost, what are you going to do? Will you do as the people of Sodom and Gomorrah did? God opened the door before He destroyed the cities. God warned them. God sent message after message after message. But the people did not listen. Only Lot, his wife, and daughters ran for their lives. But, Lot's wife looked back. Will you be like the people of old and fail to obtain God's best for your life? The door is just about to close. It is closing even as I write for some of you. The door is closing. What are you going to do? Will you step through now? The door is closing. The door is closing. Don't look back.

Maintain a Fixed Focus

When God opens the door, don't look back. Keep your eyes fixed on the Lord Jesus Christ the author of your faith (Heb. **12:2**). Keep your eyes on God. Don't look back and please don't go back. Get out of Sodom and get out now. This is your last chance. What are you going to do?

Behold, I put before you an opportunity to be blessed. Do you want to be blessed? Do you want deliverance? Do you desire change in your life? Are you ready to live for God or are you happy the way you are? I don't know about you, but I am ready. Give me Jesus! Give me Jesus now! I am walking through the open door. Behold I put before you an open door. Do it now. You will never be the same.

Conclusion

Brothers, I don't have much more to say. God is going to hold us accountable as to what we do and don't do when it comes to rightly dividing the Word of Truth. As pastors, preachers, educators, teachers, and leaders in Christendom, we should never compromise God's Word. Sometimes the assignment is difficult, but we must continue to preach the Word of God. I have experienced what the men of old experienced when it came to preaching God's Word.

There are several questions every preacher of the gospel of Jesus Christ must ask himself as he considers the ministry of preaching the Word of God with passion and conviction. He must ask, "Am I willing to fight for a divine cause? Am I fearless in times of pandemic fear in the camp of God? Do I operate by fear or by faith? Do I believe God is capable of doing for me what He has done for me in past times? Is my God a giant killer?

David believed this and much more. He defeated the giant, Goliath, with a sling and a stone. Then he gave Goliath a professional hair cut at the head level. David achieved this great feat without using another man's armor. He initially dressed in the king Saul's armor, but he refused to keep it on as he faced Goliath. David said to the king, "I cannot go in these, because I am not used to them." David took with him what he was accustomed to using when he was confronted with great challenges. David took with him—God. Once David had struck Goliath with one of his five smooth stones, he proceeded to use Goliath's own sword to remove his head. David defeated the uncircumcised stench from the camp of God. Following David's victory, the army of Goliath fled for its life. The Bible said, "When the Philistines saw that their hero was dead, they turned and ran. Then the men of Israel and Judah surged forward with a shout and pursued the Philistines to the entrance of Gath and to the gates of Ekron" (1 Sam. 17:51-52, NIV).

Preaching the Word of God is no different. When the man of God preaches the Word of God with conviction, passion, and power—things change. That is why a man of fear cannot be used by God when great faith in God is necessary. Preach the Word brother, preach it brother, preach the Word of God.

That is what I have learned to do for well over thirty-five years of teaching and preaching the Word of God. Faith always trumps fear. So, what I am saying to you my dear brother? I am saying to you that it is time for us to preach for revival and spiritual awakening. We have no power to cause a revival and an awakening, but we do have the opportunity to participate in the next move of God. Preach it brother. Preach it. Preach the Word in season and out of season.

My Sermon Notes

Subject: _____

Scripture: _____

Introduction: _____
_____
_____

1st Point
_____
_____

2nd Point
_____
_____
_____

3rd Point
_____
_____
_____

4th Point
_____
_____
_____

Conclude: With Jesus, His death, burial, resurrection and return
_____
_____

Invitation: Discipleship/Stewardship/Commitment/Obedience/Salvation
_____
_____

Schedule a Journey Workshop House of Prayer

• A One-Day Workshop

• A Weekend Prayer and Spiritual Awakening Church or Leadership or Staff Retreat

• A One Hour of Power—Can You Not Pray with Me for One Hour?

The Journey to Wholeness and Holiness: Fasting & Praying 40-Day Discipleship Devotional Book

278–Pages   Size–**6** x **9**

Do you want to be made whole? Would you like to have more peace? Are you operating at the maximum level of your God-given potential? Do you want to be made whole?

The Journey to Wholeness & Holiness: Fasting and Praying Discipleship Book

74–Pages   Size–**6** x **9**

Spiritual BONDAGE is real. The Journey to Wholeness & Holiness: Fasting and Praying Discipleship Book equips the believer to help the church respond to spiritual bondages in communities in need of Jesus.

Journey to Wholeness & Holiness: Fasting and Prayer Discipleship Workbook

102–Pages   Size–**8** ½ x **11** ½

Do you desire change in your community? Are you thirsty for what only God can do through the power of the Holy Spirit of God?

Other Conference, Prayer Events, and Options

• Spiritual Awakening and Revival Meeting
• Associational Prayer and Spiritual Awakening Vision Casting
• College and University Walls of Jericho Prayer Walking Rally
• An Inner Life Discipleship Prayer and Devotional Retreat
• Youth and Teens 40-Day Prayer and Fasting Commitment Period (Dealing with Peer Pressure: Apply Prayer Pressure)
• Church and Associational Prayer Altars, Prayer Rooms, Prayer Teaching
• The Road Block Series to Revival and Spiritual Awakening
• When Husbands and Wives Bow: Spiritual Renewal Through Prayer
• When Families Pray Together
• How to Pray Your Way Through Change
• Transforming Business Meetings into Blessing Meetings Through Prayer and Fasting
• When Children Learn How to Pray with Purpose (How to Pray for Bullies and Boohoos)
• Wholeness & Holiness: Identifying and Breaking Spiritual Bondages
• How to Pray for Rain (The Prayer Foundation of a Church Building Program and Financial Stewardship)
• How to Become A One Spirit Church Through Prayer
• How to Pray All Night

For more information concerning conferences, events, options, and resources, contact Pastor Bob Loggins at:

Robert F. Loggins, Sr. Ministries, LLC

15917 **Eagle Chase Court**
Chesterfield, MO
©2008 **RF Loggins Ministries**
Robert F. Loggins, Sr., President
Email Address: **RobertLogginsP@yahoo. com**
Website: **www. PastorLoggins. com**

Bibliography and Resources

Ackey, Alfred H. *National Baptist Hymnal*. Nashville: National Baptist Publishing Board, 1977.

Aland, Kurt, Matthew Black, Carlo M. Martini, Bruce M. Metzger, and Allen Wilgren. *The Greek New Testament*. West Germany: United Bible Societies, 1983.

Allen, Clifton. *The Broadman Bible Commentary, 1 Samuel-Nehemiah, Volume 3*. Nashville, TN: Broadman Press, 1970.

Baker, Kenneth. *The NIV Study Bible*. Grand Rapids, MI: Zondervan Publishing House, 1995.

Baker, Warren. *The Complete Word Study Old Testament, King James Version*. Chattanooga, TN: AMG Publishers, 1994.

Ball, C. J. *Nebo, the Assyrian-Babylonian god. http://books.google.com/books?id=* RTiTQSD_WusC&pg=PA169&dq=babylonian+god+Nebo&sig= N2HJ_Y2N2bBILpp 5BFJe B52XagY.

Baumann, J. Daniel. *An Introduction to Contemporary Preaching*. Grand Rapids, MI: Baker House Company, 1972.

Blackaby, Henry T. and Claude V. King. *Fresh Encounter: Experiencing God Through Prayer, Humility and a Heartfelt Desire to Know Him*. Nashville, TN: Broadman & Holman Publishers, 1996.

Bounds, E.M. *Bounds on Prayer: The Classic Collection*. Orlando, FL: Bridge-Logos, 2001.

Bromiley, Geoffrey W. *The International Standard Bible Encyclopedia*. Grand Rapids, MI: William B. Eerdmans Publishing Company, 1986.

Chapell, Bryan. *Christ-Centered Preaching: Redeeming the Expository Sermon*. Grand Rapids, MI: Baker Books, 1994.

Cone, James. *Black Theology and Black Power*. Maryknoll, NY: Orbis Books, 1969.

Dolphin, Lambert. *The Names of God.* www.dolphin.org/Names.html.

Edwards, Gene. 100 *Days in the Secret Place.* Shippensburg, PA: Destiny Image Publishers, 2001.

Elliger, K. and W. Rudolph, *Biblia Hebraica Stuttgartensia.* Stuttgart: Deutsche Bibelgesellschaft Stuttgart, 1983.

Elwell, Walter A. *The Concise Evangelical Dictionary of Theology* Grand Rapids, MI: Baker Book House, 1991.

Finney, Charles Grandison. *Experiencing Revival: A New Zeal for Life!* New Kensington, PA: Whitaker House, 1984.

Foster, Richard. *Prayer: Finding the Heart's True Home.* New York, IL: Harper Collins, 1992.

Freedman, David Noel. *Eerdmans Dictionary of the Bible.* Grand Rapids, MI: William B. Eerdmans Publishing Company, 2000.

Freeman, James M. *Manners and Customs of Bible Times.* New Kensington, PA: Whitaker House, 1996.

Frizzell, Gregory R. *Return to Holiness, A Personal and Churchwide Journey to Revival: A Biblical Guide to Daily Cleansing and Churchwide Solemn Assemblies.* Memphis: The Master Design Ministries, 2000.

Guinness, Os. *Dining With The Devil: The Megachurch Movement Flirts with Modernity.* Grand Rapids, MI: Baker Book House, 1993.

Heisler, Greg. *Spirit-Led Preaching: The Holy Spirit's Role in Sermon Preparation and Delivery.* Nashville, TN: B&H Publishing Group, 2007.

Hendriksen, William. *Survey of the Bible: A Treasury of Bible Information.* Grand Rapids, MI: Baker Books, 1976.

Henrichsen, Walter A. *Disciples Are Made Not Born: Equipping Christians to Multiply Themselves Through Ministry to Others.* Wheaton, IL: Victor Books, 1988.

Hicks, H. Beecher Jr. *Preaching Through a Storm: Confirming the Power of Preaching in the Tempest of Church Conflict.* Grand Rapids, MI: Zondervan, 1987.

Hobbs, Herschel H. *What Baptists Believe.* Nashville, TN: Broadman Press, 1964.

Hunt, T. W. and Claude V. King. *The Mind of Christ.* Nashville, TN: LifeWay Press, 1994.

Little, Paul E. *Know What You Believe.* Colorado Springs, CO: Chariot Victor Publication, David C. Cook Publication, 1999.

Lloyd-Jones, Martyn. *Revival.* Westchester, IL: Crossway Books, 1987.

Loggins, Sr. Robert F. *The Journey to Wholeness & Holiness: Fasting and Prayer.* Chesterfield, MO: RF Loggins Ministries, 2007.

McCalep, Jr., George O. *Sin in the House: Ten Crucial Church Problems with Cleansing Solutions.* Lithonia, GA: Orman Press, Inc., 1999.

Mitchell, Henry H. *Black Preaching.* San Francisco, CA: Harper & Row, 1979.

Mitchell, Henry H. *Blacking Preaching: The Recovery of a Powerful Art.* Nashville, TN: Abingdon Press, 1990.

Morris, Canon Leon. *Tyndale New Testament Commentaries The Revelation of St. John.* Grand Rapids, MI: William B. Eerdmans Publishing Company, 1981.

Murray, Andrew. *The Blood of the Cross: Christ's Blood Can Protect and Empower You!* New Kensington, PA: Whitaker House, 1981.

Murray, Andrew. *The Power of the Blood of Jesus.* New Kensington, PA: Whitaker House, 1993.

Ogilvie, Lloyd J. and Maxie D. Dunnam. *The Communicator's Commentary: Galatians, Ephesians, Phillippians, Colossians, Philemon.* Waco, TX: Word Books Publisher, 1982.

Packer, J.I. *God's Words: Studies of Key Bible Themes.* Grand Rapids, MI: Baker Book House, 1981.

Packer, J.I. and M.C. Tenney. *Illustrated Manners and Customs of the Bible.* Nashville, TN: Thomas Nelson, Inc., 1997.

Phillips, J. B. *Your God is Too Small.* New York: NY: Touchstone, 2004.

Piper, John. *Desiring God: Meditations of a Christian Hedonist*. Sisters, OR: Multnomah, 1996.

Roberts, Richard Owen. *Repentance: The First Word of the Gospel.* Wheaton, IL: Crossway Book, 2002.

Silvoso, Ed. *That None Should Perish: How to Reach Entire Cities for Christ Through Prayer Evangelism*. Ventura, CA: Regal Books, 1994.

Skinner, Kerry L. *The Joy of Repentance.* Mobile, AL: KLS/LifeChange Ministries, 2006.

Sproul, R.C. *Getting the Gospel Right: The Tie that Binds Evangelicals Together.* Grand Rapids, MI: Baker Books, 1999.

Sproul, R.C. *The Holiness of God.* Wheaton, IL: Tyndale House Publishers, Inc., 1985.

Strong, James. *The New Strong's Expanded Exhaustive Concordance of the Bible.* Nashville, TN: Thomas Nelson Publishers, 2001.

Tenney, Merrill C. *The Zondervan Picture Encyclopedia of the Bible*. Grand Rapids, MI: Zondervan Publishing House, 1976.

Tenney, Merrill C. *The Zondervan Picture Encyclopedia of the Bible*, Volume **4**, M-P. Grand Rapids, MI: Zondervan Publishing House, 1975.

Turner, J. Clyde. *Our Baptist Heritage*. Nashville: The Sunday School Board of the SBC, 1945.

Vine, W.E., Merrill F. Unger, and William White, Jr. *Vine's Complete Expository Dictionary of Old and New Testament Words: With Topical Index.* Nashville, TN: Thomas Nelson Publishers, 1996.

Walton John H., Victor H. Matthews, and Mark W. Chavalas. *The IVP Bible Background Commentary Old Testament*. Downers Grove, IL: InterVarsity Press, 2000.

Zodhiates, Spiro. *The Hebrew-Greek Key Word Study Bible, King James Version*. Chattanooga, TN: AMG Publishers, 1991.

Dictionaries

Merriam-Webster's Dictionary and Thesaurus. Springfield, MA: Merriam-Webster, Incorporated, 2006.

Scholastic Dictionary of Synonyms, Antonyms, Homonyms